Willing Workers

Willing Workers

The Work Ethics in Japan,
England, and the
United States

TAMOTSU SENGOKU

Translated by Koichi Ezaki and Yuko Ezaki

Quorum Books
Westport, Connecticut • London, England

Library of Congress Cataloging in Publication Data

Sengoku, Tamotsu, 1928–
  Willing workers.

  Includes index.
  1. Work ethic—Japan. 2. Work ethic—
England. 3. Work ethic—United States. I. Title.
HD8726.5.S37 1985   306′.36   85-9552
ISBN 0-89930-137-1 (lib. bdg. : alk. paper)

Library of Congress Catalog Card Number: 85-9552
ISBN: 0-89930-137-1

First published in 1985 by Quorum Books

Greenwood Press
A division of Congressional Information Service, Inc.
88 Post Road West, Westport, Connecticut 06881

Printed in the United States of America

The paper used in this book complies with the
Permanent Paper Standard issued by the National
Information Standards Organization (Z39.48-1984).

10 9 8 7 6 5 4 3 2 1

Copyright Acknowledgments

Willing Workers was originally published in Japanese in 1980
by Kodansha Ltd. Publishers, Tokyo, Japan

Contents

Part II. Mechanisms of Willingness to Work

Part III. Generation That Awaits Directions

Figures

Preface to English Edition

When I wrote this book in 1980, the phrase "willing worker" or "willing work" was used as a cultural key word to distinguish Japan sharply from the United States. In 1985, however, the phrase "willing worker" seems to be losing its effectiveness to differentiate between the work cultures in Japan and the United States.

Willing work, as I discuss here, originally referred to work that went beyond what is called for in the job description. In recent years, young Japanese workers, who had been becoming less involved in work, started just sticking to the job description. They are less willing to turn on the machine beforehand so that they would be able to start work on time or hold a meeting to discuss the cause of the day's junk-making.

Young Japanese workers, many of them, are not "willing workers" anymore, and they are beginning to have more things in common with American workers. Contributing to this trend is the fact that young Japanese workers have a stronger desire for freedom and that American workers have been turning back to the Protestant ethic for some time. In the third "Attitude Survey of the World Youth" by the Youth Bureau of the Prime Minister's Office, made public in 1984, we came across a historical situation. More American youth replied "work" to the question, "Which do you find more worth living for, work or leisure?" (Americans 29%, Japanese 27%). This survey has been conducted every five years, and these figures can truly be called a historical fact.

We, Japanese, think of ourselves as overworking, and Americans think of themselves as not working hard enough. The above figures are a manifestation of this attitude, and this social perception should never be overlooked. Social perceptions exert great influence on people's attitudes. Nevertheless, cultural traditions do not undergo quick change. In fact, the work that goes beyond job description never has ceased to be done, and an increase in productivity due to quality control (QC) activities seems limitless. Part II of this book deals with the cultural bases of these behaviors in detail. This discussion, I believe, will be of cultural interest to Americans and is full of suggestions for management.

Time magazine in its special issue on Japan, August 1983, carried an interesting comment about this cultural difference. It is a criticism of Japanese culture viewed by Americans, and I felt that nothing else seems to symbolize the Japanese culture so well and no other comment is more convincing. Education Professor James Shields of the City University of New York said: "The whole culture is pervaded by the ethic that with true effort you can succeed: that if you're not achieving, you haven't tried hard enough."

Every Japanese thinks that if you are not achieving, you have not tried hard enough whether in work or study. This makes up an essential part of Japanese culture—the values rooted in the consciousness of the Japanese. Interestingly enough, though, the Protestant ethic values man's effort before his talent. It might be that the two countries have something in common in their cultures.

Every Japanese thinks, too, that Japan owes her prosperity today to the assistance and guidance of the United States. It would be my immeasurable pleasure if this book contributes in some way to the greatness of the United States, which, as we say in Japanese, is requital of a favor.

Let me add, last, that I am indebted to Koichi Ezaki, one of our researchers at Japan Youth Research Institute, and Yuko Ezaki, his wife, for their strenuous efforts on the translation. Particular thanks is due, also, to William D. Heinold, who lent them a hand in refining the language.

Preface to First Edition

People who believe
That the dead never
Come back to life...
Should be here at quitting time.

A copy of the poem or phrase above caught my eye. It was on a foreman's desk in a Chicago company which I was visiting. A free interpretation might be, "If you think dead people will never come back to life, just come here when a day's work is done, and you will see that they have."

This could only be an American joke. We, Japanese, might be the only people in the whole world who would take this joke seriously and emphasize that the Americans lack willingness to work. But I personally think that there is great utility in a cross-national study of the motivation structures.

Certainly an American visitor to a Japanese factory would be astonished at the number of signs posted there. They seem to be literally everywhere. They say things like "Cooperation," "Harmony," "Responsibility," or "Reach the Goal," and so on. The visitor might say, "This is a surprise. What is this? Boy Scouts!" This candid impression of his reveals so well the sensitivity, the deeply ingrained value system, and special needs of all American workers.

The words "Cooperation" and "Responsibility" simply sound childish to him. No preaching to a man with a family, please! His remark, "What is this? Boy Scouts!" conveys to us a feeling that these are not appropriate words to hear in the factory. A factory is a place for producing goods, not a church for molding people.

From his point of view, a factory, in a sense, is a place of confrontation and contention between employer and employee for profits. Therefore, an employer should not be preaching ethics, and if he does, he is looking down on workers. He should be ashamed of it if he does, because he is already forcing work upon employees.

This book is based on our survey findings conducted at factories in Japan, the United States, and Great Britain.[1] The study was commissioned to us by the Prime Minister's Office in 1979. It was during one of the factory observations that I found the saying discussed above.

Half in jest, the author of this poem suggests that a worker is "dead" when he is working in the factory and he "revives" when the work is done. For him a factory is only a place for hard work. For this worker, work is no more than a necessary chore or even evil for maintaining life. If this is the case, how can he possibly think of it as a place for moral training or self-discipline? But a Japanese worker looks for the reason of his being or identity in hard work and even tries to improve himself by it. For him, therefore, the factory is a place for his soul to recreate itself, a place for self-improvement, and a place for spiritual training. It is only right and proper for him to work hard in the factory since he finds a real value in so doing.

This Japanese attitude toward work seems to differ fundamentally from that of the British and American workers. *Yaruki*, "willingness to work" or "drive to work," is closely related to Japanese mentality and Japanese culture. I found, while observing the factories, that the Japanese have a more challenging attitude toward what seems to be a hard task. Workers say that they are tired and want to go home, yet they stay on the job until they find a solution for problems they may have had that day. Such behavior is rarely seen in the United States or Great Britain. This very behavior of the Japanese, in fact, leads to various improvements on the production line. In one case I observed in a cardboard factory, a device was added to produce unified prints by drilling a hole in the middle of a machine and installing a spring. Workers also tried to remove dust particles using scotch tape in order to get clean prints on the cardboard. On other occasions, workers decided to come early to plan ahead for the work that had to be done. All these examples constitute a kind of "applied working," so to speak.

In actual behavior on the shop floor, there are decisive differences between Japan on one side, and the United States and Great Britain on the other. But it does not necessarily follow that behavior of this nature is a result of spiritual training or self-improvement. In fact, this self-improving type of behavior is on the decline among the Japanese. *Yaruki*, or willingness to work, has become a topic of current concern in modern Japan.

As I came to know young workers in Japanese factories, I found I could hardly apply words like spiritual training to their attitudes. In the first place, they do very little of their own accord. It seems that motivation to work arises for two reasons: either because you were given an order, or you were struck by a unique thought concerning the task. One could say there is either work that has to be done or work that is attractive enough to be done.

These two aspects of motivation are common in work psychology throughout the world. Japan is no exception. Workers are *willing* to follow orders because of a threat of penalty. If they ever get fired, they are likely to be panic-stricken. Japan differs a great deal on this point from the United States and Great Britain. Consequences of being fired are far greater for the Japanese.

Analyses by some American scholars, which will be discussed in the chapters to follow, have shown that the Japanese worker is almost completely dependent on his company. There is an almost totally work-centered structure in Japan. According to these analysts, the Japanese employment system breeds this near-complete dependence, which results in Japanese industriousness. It should be noted that the system does not motivate the workers solely by threatening and penalizing them. During any economic depression, for example, Japanese executives would rather cut their own salaries first, and only if this measure proved ineffective would they resort to asking their employees to make personal sacrifices. On the other hand, American stock-holding executives first take profits they are entitled to, and, then, if there is not enough money left to keep workers employed, they begin to lay them off. This would inevitably result in employees' losing loyalty to their company. To be sure, the Japanese employment structure and attitude create a more complete employee dependence. The company not only carries out economic functions, but also satisfies social needs of employees.

This employment structure is reinforced by employee values. Having a solid base on a functional group called company, the worker tries to satisfy his desires which center on economic stability, respect and acceptance from others, and an easy, carefree life full of interesting activities. Permanent employment via a seniority system appears to satisfy some of these desires (these seem to be common desires the world over). The seniority system has a unique standard—equality among employees who entered the company at the same period.[2] Therefore, slight differences in bonuses received may be interpreted as a threat to the need for self-respect. This need will actually enhance *yaruki* rather than suppress it because of the realization that one is either thought of highly or otherwise.

There is another particularly strong desire among the Japanese: attachment to the powerful and stable. Consequently, there is great fear among the Japanese that they might be expelled from the group. Once a worker secures a job and membership in a familylike group called company, this desire to be associated with the powerful and stable is satisfied. Should the powerful company be put on the verge of bankruptcy, he shares the fate. For example, the job shortage after the oil crisis created a lot of drive to work not only among workers freshly out of college but also among almost all Japanese. This exemplified how strong the desire for stability is among the Japanese workers.

Perhaps one desire difficult to be satisfied in the actual work situation may be self-actualization as proposed by F. W. Maslow, an American psychologist. In the real world of work, one hardly ever comes across an "interesting" and irresistibly "inviting" task. Whether we like it or not, we have a system of giving and receiving orders. If one fails to obey orders or measure up to expectations, he can hardly have self-actualized.

Working because one "has to" is slightly different from working because one "wants to." When one works because the work is "irresistibly interesting," his psychological reaction is close to the ideal of *yaruki*, willingness to work.

In the case of the Japanese, it seems to me that *yaruki* cannot be measured by the yardstick of personal interest in the job. When we look at actual Japanese workers, interesting or uninteresting jobs are not the deciding factor. They seem to be motivated by the fact that "the job is there." This is totally different from the American or British way of deciding on the basis of individual job circumstances, regardless of the number of jobs to be done.

The central theme of this book lies here: Why is a Japanese worker willing to work just because "the job is there"? The theme relates to the value system ingrained deeply in the mind of the Japanese. It is very difficult to pinpoint exactly. Most of our involuntary actions are motivated by deeply ingrained values, a part of our consciousness. Only through a comparative study with the motivation to work of other cultures will it ever be clarified. It is for this reason a survey of the factories of a similar kind was carried out in Japan, the United States, and Great Britain.

Our major finding was that the Japanese work willingly simply because "the work is there." Why is this so in Japan? I just want to point out here that, when the work is conceived to be there, accomplishing the task means a great deal for the Japanese.

I would like to review briefly the contents of the book. In Part I, sociological aspects of the organization or work from the comparative perspective are discussed, such as employment system and social structure, which are considered to be surroundings for or sources of *yaruki*. In Part II, the underlying human psychology, the psychological mechanism of willingness to work, is dealt with. In Part III, *yaruki* among the youth is discussed.

Actual examples and episodes were obtained directly through observation and interviews. Originally, I had managers and heads of
personnel departments in mind as readers. But general principles are
derived from actual comparisons, and I have so arranged the material
that I think readers in general will find the book of much interest and
concern.

PART I

Employment Structure and Willingness to Work

1

Hourly Workers

LATE ANYWAY, WHY NOT TAKE A CIGARETTE BREAK?

The following incident occurred while we were observing T. Company in England. Mr. Robertson, who came to work late, headed straight to the rest quarters. What is more, he started enjoying his cup of tea and smoking his pipe. To us this behavior seemed to be a serious offense. Had he started a one-man strike?

This incident occurred at the beginning of our survey, and we knew we had discovered a really interesting phenomenon. What was it that was driving him to such action? Our common sense tells us that when late, one should rush to one's workplace. One should be ashamed in one's heart and show it in behavior. Mr. Robertson's reply to our queries was unexpectedly simple. He was late to work by two minutes, and because he is paid by fifteen-minute units, fifteen minutes' worth of pay would be subtracted from his salary. Consequently, if Mr. Robertson had gone right to work, he would have worked thirteen minutes for nothing. He chose to go straight to the rest quarters instead.

Everybody will understand Robertson's negative attitude about "working for nothing." It is not only England that suffers from this malaise. Our Japanese youth today could be much worse. Theirs is a generation that does little more than await directions. If people do not work during work hours unless instructed, they are mere parasites and "stealing" their salary, to say nothing of working for nothing.

In Japan workers will not have worked for nothing when late to work. On the contrary, they will gain what they are not entitled to for the two minutes they are late. The reason is simple; the Japanese pay system is based on a monthly salary. R. Company in Japan, for example, which produces corrugated cardboard boxes like T. Company in England, will not cut wages even when their employees are several hours late.

A crucial difference between the two companies is the wage system.

Employees' reactions differ almost diametrically. An English worker smokes his pipe leisurely while a Japanese worker dashes to his workplace.

No doubt the wage system has a great deal to do with willingness to work. Workers under hourly wage systems work "by the hour" as the dictionary defines. Those who engage in actual production in the factories in the United States and England are *all* hourly workers. In Japan, with the exception of temporary workers, almost all are monthly workers who work "by the month."

These days, many housewives work part time and so do college students. A part-time worker only has to be at a certain place for a certain amount of time. Generally, his presence is confirmed by a timeclock. Whether sales go up or down makes no difference to his pay. We can assume that Japanese part-time workers are similar to hourly workers in England and the United States. The supervisor always has to be on the spot to tell them what to do.

The so-called generation that awaits directions[1] is pressured to change its values, even though superficially, through training sessions and on-the-job training (OJT). But the nucleus of their values, like an indomitable flow of history, might be suggestive of *yaruki* among the Japanese workers in the days to come. Training sessions and OJT might be wasted efforts, going against history. Ten or twenty years from now we might be saying that this certainly is the case. (The value system of the generation that awaits directions will be dealt with in detail in Part III.)

Back to the present, let us analyze Mr. Robertson's behavior. As long as we look at his behavior through the mind of the Japanese, his going straight to the rest quarters means that he has no willingness to work, and the wage system is the direct cause of his lack of willingness—the system that takes away the sum for fifteen minutes from his total wages. We called him an hourly worker, but actually he is a quarter-hourly worker. He is in quite a different position from a Japanese worker. Of course, the monetary reward system is not all there is to it when we talk about a real motive for having much drive to work. What comes to my mind offhand is zeal for work rather than money. What supports the popularity of the Japanese TV program "Netchu-jidai" (The Generation of Zeal)[2] with young people is the spirit shown in actions of sacrifice by the hero, beyond what is called for by his job—which I see as zeal.

The system that allows working for nothing and the desire to feel zeal for work represents "structure" and "desire" centering around *yaruki*. They are indeed interrelated. Culture supports the social structure of *yaruki*. Meanwhile, the traditional Japanese social system within the field of industrial society, namely that of the seniority system and permanent employment, has been greatly shaken since the oil crisis. A change in the social structure has transformed angry youth into submissive ones. Here is an example of structural change bringing about a change in the value system and eventually a change in one's desire.

Social structure and cultural values are interdependent. These two aspects have to be taken up in order to discuss "willingness" to work. It does not mean however, that they are composed of entirely different principles. Japanese social structure and the Japanese value system are founded on the traditional Japanese culture and are characteristic of the desires of the Japanese.

The basic elements of drive to work are psychological, such as personal motivation and self-image. Reward and promotion act as stimuli, but, unlike desires, they are formalized and systematized and leave room for selection. There is a tendency, for instance, among young people to put less value on promotion. Rather than going up the ladder of promotion, these youths are trying to find substantial value in leisure activities or pleasure-seeking. They have equally attractive alternatives between promotion and leisure activities. Unless they see some value in promotion, they are not willing to make any effort, nor are they willing to work.

It is fruitless, therefore, to tell youths who find their life goal in leisure activities that they can achieve promotion by exerting their energies in work. A stimulant for a high position can either be effective or ineffective depending upon one's values. Desires—such as economic stability or respect from others—are naturally innate in man, inclusive of the ones developed later in life. Everybody aspires toward stability and respect. Everybody craves money and status.

Everyone is eager to satisfy personal wants. But a mere stimulus on wants does not always act as a motivator. Each person has the option of accepting such motivating factors as wages and promotion. They are weighed and calculated. Therefore, the worker sees a certain effort producing a certain result. Accordingly, some choose work, others choose leisure activities. The crucial factor is the value system.

A diversity of values, or a change in values, nullifies the expectation for promotion. This is a grave fact. We cannot neglect the emergence of a generation that thinks that it is ridiculous to sacrifice self so much just to become a section chief and that it makes much more sense to do things that please themselves. A diversity of values not only causes the whole work system to be ineffective but also affects people's own desires. Desires may be more or less unchangeable, but their intensity is greatly affected.

Some desires are innate and others acquired. A change in values influences the latter. In a sense, value system is the rationale behind the scenes. It sets a standard for deciding whether A or B is more valuable. In Japan today, one hardly ever meets with the value that sacrifices self for the benefit of the public or nation. The value system that requires sacrifices for one's company, section chief, or superiors is also on the decline. The value that sacrifices present for future is losing popularity. Values change with time, and one's desires are affected by it. The study of motivation structure, especially among youth, will have to lead to the study of their values.

Social institutions such as a raise system, bonus system, promotion system, job rotation system (which has a lot to do with fast promotion), etc., become factors in employment structure and social structure only after their repeated observance. These institutions, therefore, must be analyzed along with value changes.

We are likely to find out in the international comparative study on *yaruki* that the institutions, especially those of employment structure and social structure, play a great role. Clues can be found for developing a new Japanese motivation structure to work. Social institutions are the most basic stimulants to various human desires. Stimulants to *yaruki* vary greatly from country to country and culture to culture. These differences are shown most clearly in institutions. Thus, we shall first deal with the meaning of such social institutions. And in the latter part of the book, we will move to the analyses of values and psychological factors.

COMPANY BUS VS. PUSHERS

In England, company buses are becoming very popular for commuting. Our survey results show that 15% of employees commute by company bus, which comes to the community square to pick them up. Compared to Japan, housing and workplaces are located relatively close to one another. Even in the countryside many workers live in a community where there is a factory. Moreover, blue-collar workers and white-collar workers often live in different communities. The bus can pick up most of the workers by going to the blue-collar community.

In Japan, kindergarten buses are operated in much the same way as the British company bus. Of course the British company cannot force the workers to board the bus (as is the case with crying or shouting children). So when the bus comes, a worker himself must decide whether to go to work.

The company bus was devised as the last resort in response to a high rate of absenteeism. At one time, absenteeism in British factories was as high as 15%, five times as high as the average of 3% in Japan. In America, the figure is not so high as in Britain, but it is becoming problematic. In his book *Wheels*, Arthur Hailey talks about such a problem in an automobile factory:

Mondays and Fridays in auto plants were management's most harrowing days because of absenteeism. Each Monday, more hourly paid employees failed to report for work than on any other normal weekday; Friday ran a close second. It happened because after paychecks were handed out, usually on Thursday, many workers began a long boozy or drugged weekend, and afterward, Monday was a day for catching up on sleep or nursing hangovers.[3]

They say that the introduction of company buses helped to decrease the absenteeism rate to about 8% in England. Another interesting practice is an award of a bonus for punctuality. At T. Company 5% of the wage is added as a bonus if a worker reports for work on time. He has a bus come for him, and he gets a bonus. This is really class treatment. Something bothered me about this, so I asked what would happen if the bus were late and workers did not get to work on time? I pressed this point with the personnel manager, and he assured me that such a case had not yet occurred. When I insisted on the possibility, he said that he would still pay the bonus.

To begin with, people initiate their motivation or drive to work when they arrive at work. Unless the worker arrives, there is no point in talking about *yaruki*. But what drives people just to arrive at work? Money? Yes. Responsibility for the work and company? Yes. But no one asks himself these questions each day before coming to work. So what really drives people to go to work? A close inquiry must reveal some aspects of *yaruki*. And if what drives people to go to work is not tangible enough, perhaps the question, "What bothers you when you are absent from work?" might be more accessible. This is why we picked absenteeism rate as one of the themes of our survey.

Now back to the Japanese scene. Once they become new recruits, even those happy and carefree ex-students try as much as they can to be on time and not to be absent from work. It is almost a legend that salaried workers who were born between 1926 and 1934 (the first decade of Showa)[4] prided themselves on crawling to work on all fours (read tremendous effort) even with the worst possible hangovers.

An English cartoonist became famous by drawing what he saw at Shinjuku Station in Tokyo. The cartoon was titled "The Pusher."[5] It was simply inscrutable and strange in his English eyes that people had to struggle and sweat blood in rush hours only to go to work. Why all these pains? They do not get 5% bonuses for their effort. In spite of this struggling and blood-sweating, the absenteeism rate in Japan is very low—a mere 3%. The 3% figure suggests that people come to work even when sick.

By the way, company buses do exist in Japan. Kawaguchi Factory of R. Company, for instance, is located about ten to fifteen minutes by bus from Kawaguchi Station. Every morning, company buses from different companies line up in front of the station to pick up employees. The bus stop is even coordinated according to the arrival time of each bus. They do not come close to the worker's residence as in the case of the British company. Employees struggle and fight their way on the crowded trains as far as the station.

Employees are quite dismayed if they miss the company bus. The only choice then is to take a taxi. The fare could jump from 730 to 800 yen if there is a traffic jam. "Don't miss the bus!" manifests the feelings of the Japanese, since the taxi fare is out of the question. "In Japan, workers pay the taxi fare out of their own pocket to come to work, if they miss the bus," I said to the personnel manager of T. Company in England. Of course, coming to work on time this way will not get them 5% bonuses. This was absolutely beyond the comprehension of Mrs. Bird, the personnel manager, who replied: "Employees pay the taxi fare? Don't they come to the company to earn their wages?"

I could write a whole book to appease Mrs. Bird. Anybody will be under the impression that British workers get a more favorable treatment as far as the comparison on commuting goes. But in Japan, workers will never be cut fifteen minutes' worth of wages from their salary when they are two minutes late. This is a crucial difference between hourly workers and monthly workers. Hourly workers are, in fact, part-timers. A supermarket, hiring hourly workers, will not pay bonuses even if they make a huge profit. Part-timers will not get promoted no matter how hard they work. Part-timers get their hourly wages re-gardless of the gains of the store. Even if sales drop and eventually the store goes out of business, it will not affect the pay of part-timers. There is some similarity between hourly workers in England and part-timers in Japan. They are not committed to their company. It is literally not their business. They are outsiders.

A survey by the French government shows very well the value system along this line. "Do you feel that your company's business has a great deal to do with your income?" As high as 62% answered "no."[6] On the other hand, in reply to the next question, "Would you work for the same company you now work for if you were to do it over again?" 68% answered "yes." Hourly workers expect very little from the company to start with, but that does not mean that they are dissatisfied with it.

Whether one is committed to the company or not makes a difference between getting a 5% bonus out of commuting by company bus and paying one's own taxi fare. And a major institutional difference is whether one is paid hourly or monthly. The mentality of an hourly worker is close to that of a housewife who works part time in Japan. She uses her earnings as her own spending money or for the family budget. Her true workplace as a housewife is at home. The same logic holds for a British hourly worker. His real self is at home, in a man's castle, enjoying gardening.

This value system that assumes a workplace and self as tentative does not match the Japanese culture. In traditional Japanese culture, "even a chance meeting is preordained." We need a system of sharing the pleasures and pains of life even in a workplace, and a monthly wage and permanent employment system satisfies this need best.

The younger generation has been revising this system. While they look for unity, they dislike being the party concerned as discussed by Keigo Okonogi.[7] "Keeping oneself cool" is characteristic of them, and they dislike being involved and sharing profits, pleasures, or pains. The value system which avoids being the party concerned would mean a lesser sense of belonging.

Youths yearn strongly for comfortable stability, but they lack tenacity necessary for its fulfillment. They cope with things one step removed so that they will stay intact and so that they can change their stance any time. They will not be canvassing for the company unless they are fully assured of their success. They will not sacrifice their precious time, let alone their own pocket money.

They have begun to hold a value system that is in line with the hourly wage system. They are losing a sense of commitment and involvement that goes with the monthly wage and permanent employment systems. They are in a small measure British as far as desires and values are concerned—not getting paid when absent from work and not getting paid unless productivity is improved. The day might come soon when the American and British systems find their way into Japan.

ONLY THE BRAVE TAKE THE WHOLE PAID HOLIDAY

The system that links the firms and employees together has a lot to do with *yaruki*. In America and in Britain, it means, in principle, very little other than that people get paid $5 or 2 pounds per hour. There are such things as the seniority system, which secures job rights and a welfare system. But I would have to say that a company-employee linkage is stronger among the Japanese.

This "tie" between a firm and employees is a system of assimilation or unification of the basic values that support the relationship. A Japanese worker will think that the company's loss ends up being his own loss, while an American worker will think, in many cases, that it has nothing to do with him; and a British worker will even think in some cases that the company's profit is his loss, for he feels that the company makes profits by exploiting him.

"How did you use your time while you were absent from work?" was the question we used to clarify this point.

This question tended to put Japanese white-collar workers on the defensive, which aroused our interest. Their response stood out in sharp contrast to the one made by some Americans, "I was working on another job."

The rate of the workers who use up their paid vacations in Japan is about 40%, which means that most of their absences are officially recognized, paid vacations which are an exercising of one's own right.[8] What one does during a paid vacation should be none of the company's business. To Japanese subjects of the survey, however, it seems that this was not true. The question stung their conscience.

In Japan, "sick in bed" is reported 10% more often among those who work in marketing departments or by white-collar workers, than among engineers and technicians. No proof exists that white-collar workers become sick at a rate higher than others. We concluded that white-collar workers used sickness as an excuse rather than a reason.

Indeed, to be absent from the company, sickness sounds better than a trip to Hawaii (which is so popular among young female workers). Since sickness has no immediate connection with one's personal will and is beyond one's control, it is a legitimate excuse.

Sometimes a careful study of data reveals an unexpected mode of life behind the scenes. The fact that Japanese workers, especially white-collar workers, use sickness as an excuse does have a meaning of no small consequence.

Why use sickness as an excuse for a paid vacation? Why not a trip to Hawaii? In Japan people think it is sinful, even if a worker is exercising the right, to be absent from work. The question "How did you use your time while you were absent from work?" to be sure, stings their conscience. If they have no sense of guilt whatsoever, they should have responded fairly and squarely like some Americans who explicitly said that they "worked at other places" while absent from the company.

The content of absenteeism was examined in detail in our survey of workers in corrugated cardboard factories in Japan, the United States, and Britain and is illustrated in figure 1. We asked: "The last time you were absent from work, was it a paid vacation, or not?" The rate of taking an unpaid vacation, nonexercising of one's right, was as high as 67% in S. Company in the United States, 37% in W. Company in the United States, and 27% in T. Company in Britain, while it was less than 2% in Japan.

An hourly worker resembles a part-timer who is paid so much per

Figure 1. Japanese Take Fewer Paid Vacation Days

"The last time you were absent from work, was it a paid vacation?"
(Percentages reflect "yes" answers.)

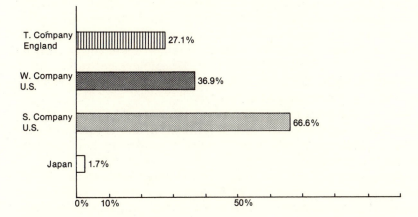

hour. If one worked at other jobs, it might mean that the other jobs paid him better than his own company for a day's work. We often hear that a taxi driver earns more by doing business independently. In Italy many drivers get their basic wages by taking out the company cars and using their own cars for making extra profits.

Hourly workers in America and Britain seem to have no relationship with their company other than getting paid so much per hour. They, of course, make full use of the benefits of paid holidays. When one has enough savings and is sure of making both ends meet, they absent themselves, unpaid.

The effect of absence on oneself, and not its effect on the company, is the only standard of judgment in the case of absenteeism in the United States and Britain. This is an American and British basis for judgment. Whether the company needs him or not doesn't matter, nor does the worker consider the amount of work that has to be done.

Underneath this value judgment is an hourly worker system. What price will a worker set on his labor, and for what price per hour will the company buy it? What links the two together is an hourly sales contract. When business diminishes and no labor is necessary, the company will lay off or fire workers, since there is no need of buying labor at a time of no work. Workers themselves keep this in mind, too. They both find no value maintaining a relationship on a permanent basis. They certainly have no sense of sharing hardships. A work system of buying and selling labor by the hour is best suited for them.

Hourly worker systems have rigorous rules which are based on the premise that workers lack *yaruki*. No worker is supposed to or expected to work voluntarily because this is not a hardship-sharing system. Workers do not work on their own initiative. They just follow the lead of their superiors. Under this system, workers are dismissed when they fall well below the prescribed level of production. Many absences without notice is also good reason for firing. These and other wage-cut rules go with the system. No other threat is equal to unemployment. It is the strongest possible incentive to work. Unemployment rate is high in both the United States and Britain. Firing procedures are thus clearly agreed upon with the labor union.

Under the Japanese system, when one takes a paid day off with an excuse of sickness, one is beginning to suffer from lack of *yaruki*. Workers are not fired even if there is no work. The workers and the firm share the same fate.

Workers work of their own accord in the Japanese system, and all superiors have to do is to take the initiative and set a good example. There is no need for giving directions as a rule. Unlike America and Britain, there is no definite procedure for firing after so many warnings. All employees, in a sense, give warning to each other.

We cannot deny, though, that this system is going through a transition because of a change in values among the youth. They tend not to work unless directed, and they do not always comply with orders, initiatives, and good examples from their superiors. They tend to go home even when it seems that overtime is unavoidable for the next day's program. Such cases are becoming too numerous to mention. In many work situations, they stay overtime only when bosses promise a drink on the way home. The traditional Japanese system is no longer functional due to this change in values. It is worth noting that there appear to be new Japanese who do not respond to changes in surrounding situations. This, in fact, might imply a change in the Japanese themselves.

NO AWOL AMONG THOSE BORN IN THE FIRST DECADE OF SHOWA

Indications are prevalent that the values of Japanese youth are becoming similar to those of American youth. It may be imminent, also, in this context, that a comparative study among American and British systems and the traditional Japanese system be done.

Absenteeism without leave (AWOL) and wildcat strikes are probably typical of the English malaise. In hourly worker systems, because labor is bought and sold per hour, it is naturally weak in permanence or continuity as compared to a lifetime employment system, to say the

**Figure 2.   Americans Are Absent from Work More Often without
Notification**

"Did you notify the company the last time you were absent?"
(Percentages reflect "no" answers.)

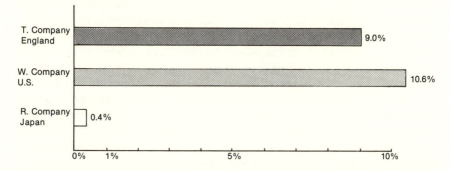

least. On the other hand, work demands continuity as a premise as
long as it stays organizational. The hourly worker system finds itself
in a dilemma here. When firms run out of work, they have the advantage of discharging employees and managing with reduced manpower.
It is obviously desirable that employees stay on the job when the work
requires longer periods for its completion. S. Company in the United
States is endeavoring to lower the turnover rate to 2% a month. Translated to a yearly measure, this means that more than 20% of the
employees quit in a year. This is too high. A priority order from the
personnel department to the foremen, therefore, is, "Talk to the workers." Talk, and you will know them and like them.

I reported previously that an hourly worker does not base his judgment on whether the company needs him or wants him for some amount
of work. Absenteeism without leave, which is said to be one of the
English problems, and wildcat strikes reveal well that workers base
their judgment solely on their own convenience. "Did you notify the
company the last time you were absent?" was the question we used to
clarify this point.

The result is shown in figure 2. About 10% of American and British
workers are absent without notice. Because many of their absences are
days off without pay, as we saw before, the figure is not to be treated
lightly. Company's convenience is disregarded, so can we conclude that
their decision is strongly based on their own convenience? This carries
some weight when considering behaviors within an organization. Will
people react or do something in response to the conditions surrounding
them and others, or will their self-assertion precede regardless of
conditions?

All three factories in figure 2 are in the business of production and sales of corrugated cardboard. In order to see what absenteeism without leave signifies, let us look at actual work. All the plants operate three eight-hour shifts.

The key operation in the plants is that of pasting cardboard together. Three pieces of cardboard are glued together to form a specified "board strength." The secret of strength lies in its "corrugation." The machine itself is called a corrugate machine. Much alertness and precise judgment are required of an operator of a corrugate machine. Not one of the factories is provided with a spare of such a costly machine; therefore, the machine is operated twenty-four hours a day. No time can be lost due to machine malfunction or a break between the cardboards. Too much glue creates loss of time for drying; too little glue means insufficient adhesion of the cardboards. Thickness of the cardboard makes the whole difference. In the case of thin cardboard, the machine can be operated at high speed because the glue dries fast. But the speed cannot be too high because thin cardboard may tear. If this happens, opertion has to be stopped while the two ends are fastened together. Circumstances differ from case to case, but the production stops for about three minutes in a Japanese factory, about seven minutes in an American factory, and about ten minutes in a British factory. It amounts to a considerable loss.

A corrugate machine operator is a key employee in the factory. He has to be alert and able to make accurate judgments in order to qualify for the job. All operators are always cooperating and keeping time with each other, so that they are prepared to take tactical measures. Once in trouble, all their physical and mental energy is put together to take the best possible measure. Amidst the heat for the drying, they challenge the limit of efficiency with their watchful eyes on meters and the flow of cardboard. An operator of the corrugate machine is an attacker, challenger, and person in the spotlight.

There are other operations going on in the factory besides pasting, such as printing customers' names and making creases in accordance with box sizes. This process called box making is where another battle for speed is being fought.

One absence in the factory has a serious influence on the whole operation. In case of absence, the place is filled by a substitute from another section or by a relief from another shift. This means that an absence in the first shift is filled by a relief from the second shift, and so on. Consequently, everybody in the factory comes to be well informed of how his absence affects others.

Thus, the Japanese workers in a cardboard factory are reluctant to believe that 10% of their counterparts in America and England absent themselves without notice. Indeed, one absence without notice might induce a cancellation of the whole operation. Before work starts, a proper number of workers is assigned where necessary. Workers in Japan go directly to their posts, as they have their own preassigned spots. They do not need daily instructions for assignment of posts. Circumstances cannot be the same when there is a 15% absenteeism without notice. A roll call will be inevitable to find out how many are missing.[9] The problem does not end here. The impact of absence depends on how the company is notified. Notification is notification, whether it comes on that very afternoon or several days in advance. But precise arrangements for a substitute can be made if an absence is reported several days in advance. It would be of help if notification came right before a day's work starts. If notification comes after a day's work has started, it is much worse, and a day's program could be seriously delayed.

Notification before the absence is different from notification of absence after a day's work has started, which should be classified as an absence without notice. Let us examine this internationally on different levels. We compare the rate of "several days in advance" and that of "on that day."

Comparison of Absenteeism by Type of Notification

Company	Several Days in Advance	On That Day	No Notice
R. Co. (Japan)	69.1%	23.1%	0.6%
W. Co. (U.S.)	41.9%	27.3%	10.6%
T. Co. (England)	71.4%	10.5%	9.0%

T. Company in England fares the best. R. Company in Japan has few absences without notice, but has more notifications "on that day" than T. Company in England. This is a perplexing finding.

We asked production chiefs of several companies in Japan to clarify the matter. No one knows in advance if one will get sick or if an emergency will come up. It stands to reason, therefore, that workers make a decision to be "off duty" on that day. People do not predetermine sickness. Even so, the percentage of "sudden illness" in the Japanese companies in comparison with that of T. Company in England is too high. Production chiefs admit that it is "fishy."

We have evidence that is indicative. Many workers give sickness and family expedience as their reason for absence in Japan and in Britain. Sickness rate is higher in Japan, and family expedience is overwhelmingly high in England. We cannot declare that the Japanese catch cold or fall ill at a higher rate than the English. Besides, English hourly workers do not have to use an excuse for their absence. We, therefore, assume their responses to be genuine.

What kind of people decide to be absent on that day? We further examined those who absented themselves. Many of the offenders, if I may call them that, are young females engaged in office work. They notify the company of their absence "on the day." But there are few offenders on the shop floor. Among those few, a difference is seen between generations. I can claim that not a single offender exists among those born in the first decade of Showa.

Production chiefs on the shop floor unanimously say that these offenders do notify on the day, but they call early in the morning so that their absence will cause the least obstruction to the day's program. A production chief said, "Hardly any inconvenience to us."

Japanese youngsters are very anxious to get away from work. Young female workers are the first to leave. They are quite brave and determined, while young boys tend to hold back. These boys, instead, use sickness as an excuse and make an early morning call so that there will be the least hindrance to the business. They are making a compromise between work and leisure activities. Those born in the first decade of Showa have not been courageous enough even to use sickness as an excuse. History of *yaruki* is being rewritten mainly by young female workers. In a word, this phenomenon is a transition from monthly wage earners to hourly workers.

2

Meritocracy

MR. WRIGHT, A GREAT HAND AT MAKING JUNK

"Wright is terrible. All he makes is 'junk.' " A supervisor on the shop floor, wearing a white gown like a doctor thus complained. The scene takes place in C. Plant of W. Company in New Jersey. But what sort of "junk"? We had to see it. Thanks to the supervisor, we came face-to-face with the junk and its maker, Mr. Wright. It was exactly correct to call it "junk." The product names were printed too far to one side of the carton so only half of the company's name could be seen on the cardboard. Moreover, the prints were slanted. One got the impression that the goods were inferior and the company was perhaps going out of business. Labels have to be neat and properly balanced. These could hardly be called salable. The supervisor added that Mr. Wright often produced this kind of junk through carelessness.

We need to become acquainted with how the printing operation is done. Three pieces of cardboard are glued together to get a boardlike sturdiness. Sizes differ in accordance with the prospective contents. A variety of customers demand a variety of sizes and dimensions. Cartons of different sizes are manufactured for each user. Lines are preset in proper positions to be folded into a box. The customer's name and brand name are printed on it before folding.

Mr. Wright handles this printing process. All he has to do is load the cardboard onto the printer. The machine has to be kept supplied, turned off when all stock is gone, and the ink supply replenished. These tasks require no special skill. But here is this junk. What motivates him to do it? A look at the printing process answered the question. The printer and cardboard have different widths. The printer is wider than the inserted cardboard. This allows the cardboard to slide freely to the right or left, resulting in oblique prints. An image of "rotten cans and company going out of business" is thus born.

We understood what the supervisor meant by Wright's carelessness. The operator has to be watchful enough so that the cardboard stays in position. He has to use his hands when the cardboard begins to slip away. The printing process is fairly automatic. When as much cardboard as possible is loaded onto the printer, it moves forward one-by-one automatically. What probably happens is that Mr. Wright gets so relaxed after the machine is fed with the cardboard and starts its operation that his attention gets turned away from the machine.

After looking at Mr. Wright's junk, we became interested in what is done in a similar Japanese company. Do they produce prints like Wright's? How is the operator handling the job? What we found was a slight surprise: no junk. Is the operator giving constant attention to the cardboard without even a moment of inattention? No. The machine is ignored while the printing is going on. The secret was simply a surprisingly little gadget.

The printer used is wider than the cardboard. The case is absolutely no different from Mr. Wright's: a variety of customers and a variety of sizes. They both use the same printers. The only difference was the installation of a spring in the hole drilled through the side of the machine. It makes the machine keep the cardboard in a fixed position, which avoids irregular printing.

The spring was not originally provided as part of the machine. It was a device improvised by a man named Nozaki, who is in charge of the process. "It's what everybody thinks. There must be some ways to improve the machine. Not just me. It simply occurred to me that the use of hands is a waste of labor, and I came up with this gadget. Don't get too excited about it. You will see several other devices of the sort." He was right. Several devices were seen, among which was the use of scotch tape to take invisible dust off the surface of the cardboard.

Junk causes materials and personnel costs to go to waste. Doing nothing might be even better, in that it would at least save materials and electricity, if not personnel expenses. The most inefficient thing to do is to produce junk; nothing is accomplished. Suppose one person works at one printer for the same amount of time in both C. Plant of W. Company in America and K. Plant of R. Company in Japan. A big difference will be seen between the two.

It is often said of meritocracy that the seniority system in Japan treats employees equally regardless of merit, and that it has no function to instill *yaruki*. In America, on the contrary, an adoption of meritocracy functions as an incentive toward more merit.

The case here is only of the printing of cardboard, but no assertion can be made, it seems, that American meritocracy has a better function in merit-making than the Japanese seniority system. Can we say, rather, that the seniority system comprises an incentive mechanism to willingness to work? Five or six new cars out of a hundred, in America, need repair within a year, but the equivalent figure in Japan is only 0.4 cars out of a hundred. Also, 2 or 3% of integrated circuits produced in the United States is defective, but the rate is only one tenth of that in Japan. It has almost become common knowledge that Japan is a step ahead in the field of quality control.[1]

DISAPPOINTMENT OF AMERICANS

In reply to the question of why Japanese products have a good market in the United States, the following article appearing in the *New York Times* provides one answer. The article discussed a slowdown in productivity in the United States:

The overwhelming majority of Americans are disheartened by the performance and direction of the national economy. This conclusion emerged from last week's New York Times/CBS News survey and was reinforced by an independent poll conducted by Garth Associates for the conference on United States competitiveness, held at Harvard University last weekend. The Garth survey showed the following:

Ninety percent of Americans believe the economy is headed in the wrong direction, and 87 percent believe that drastic steps are needed to strengthen the economy.

Two-thirds see the crisis as fundamental, not stemming from minor sources nor only from the energy problem.

Of those who think the nation is in crisis, 58 percent expect it to last three years or more and 23 percent say it will last five years or more. Only 13 percent expect it to be over in a year.

Two-thirds of Americans believe the United States is losing ground, both economically and militarily, to other countries....

The Harvard conference, which was sponsored by the United States Senate Subcommittee on International Trade, the New York Stock Exchange and Harvard University, dramatized these national anxieties but failed to explain the underlying causes.

Prof. Zvi Grilleches of Harvard, reviewing the data and analyses of declining American productivity, concluded that there was "almost no agreement on the sources of the slowdown." There are plenty of potential villains, including the decline in real research and development expenditures; declines in the rate of investment in new capital equipment; changes in the labor force, with more young people and women; Government regulation; the rise in energy prices; inflation, and errors of measurement.[2]

Discussion is going on, in the midst of an economic crisis in America, especially on why American goods are inferior in quality, which is conspicuously shown in the slowdown in productivity and in the dispute over automobile trade. The quoted article is but one example. Why on earth does productivity slow down, and why are inferior goods produced in America? Why do the Japanese and the Germans produce superior

Figure 3.   How Factory Organization Affects Technological Innovation and Productivity

Size of Product Demand

	Low ──────→ High	
Low	Type I	Type II
High	Type III	Type IV

Technological Sophistication ↓

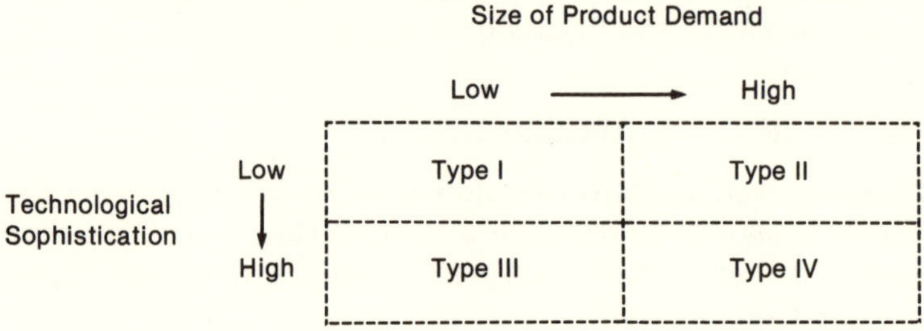

goods? Studies are under way to explore this national concern from every possible perspective. The American government itself seems to take a growing interest in the study of innovation and improvement in productivity. As part of this concern, a Rutgers University team (Koya Azumi, Jerald Hage, Frank Hull, and myself) was commissioned by the National Science Foundation to investigate a research project titled "Technical-Market Context, Organizational Design, and Industrial Innovation." Our proposal included a comparative study with Japan, which had been entrusted to us by that team.[3]

The objective of this study is to see how factory organizations affect technical innovation and productivity (see figure 3). Here factory organizations are examined through two axes. The horizontal axis shows size of product demand, and the vertical axis, technological sophistication. The following four types are presupposed out of these two axes. These organizational types are derived from organizational factors by John H. Freeman.[4]

Type I presupposes, for example, traditional industries that require professional craftsmanship, such as clothing, furniture, housing, and restaurants. The demand for a product is not great in this category because tastes play an important part. It does not require a sophisticated technology and is not suited to mass production. We can assume R & D (research and development) of Type I to be low.

Concrete examples of Type II are industries like automobile, glass, cigarette, rubber, and cement production. Their technological innovation dates back to the past. The present stress is on innovation in the process, rather than innovation in the products. Technological sophistication is low, and scale of production is high. R & D is average and will be centralized.

Type III includes industries like electronics, precision apparatus, radioisotope, and medical appliances. Their ratio of expenditure on research and development in proportion to capital expense is high.

Quality speaks more than cost. Under these organizational circumstances, R & D has to be decentralized, and attention will have to be directed to the process.

Type IV will be in many cases what type III will grow into. Systematic research aimed at innovation of technological fundamentals will be conducted, but many problems will arise in aspects of its scale and facilities. No concrete examples can be given at this moment, but some chemical industries might belong to this type.

Innovation will bring about new products and a change in the process, which will eventually lower the price, improve quality, or lead to production of superior products. Centralization of research and development works favorably toward innovation of technological fundamentals, which, however, runs a high risk. Decentralization will make it easier to cope with varied needs. An attitude by top management, whether they have a deep concern about R & D or are willing to take risks, exerts much influence.

The following are possible hypotheses:

1. The more concentration and diversification of specialists, the higher the speed of innovation.
2. The more specialization in research and development, the higher the speed of innovation.
3. The more encouragement from management on innovation, the higher the speed of innovation.
4. The more experiences in innovation in the past, the more prospects of innovation in technological fundamentals.

The problem is, though, what is the basis for a high level of expertise when we talk about technological level or specialists? Another basic problem is whether people will manifest or demonstrate their full competence just because they are on a high technological level or have the expertise. This will bring us back to the question of *yaruki*. Will a comparative study between Japanese and American factories without the element of willingness to work reveal to us the difference? The researchers expressed major differences of opinion and objections over this point in preparing for our survey.

To take an example of productivity in the chart, Type II, a large-scale mass production type, is high in productivity, although it is low in technological level. No one will object on this point. An automobile plant was considered as a typical Type II industry. However, Japanese cars surpass those made in America in quality while productivity remains high. As pointed out by Professor Kenichi Odawara of Sophia University, American cars cannot be put on the market in Japan because of their poor assembly unless they are completely disassembled, then reassembled, which inevitably doubles the price.[5]

If we classify the technological level of the automobile industry as low, the survey result will not reflect the quality of Japanese cars. Here lies a controversy. The technological aspect obviously has to be divided into two parts. One is the difference in technological level, and the other is the application of the technology. There is a split in opinion on both points.

One view suggests that Japanese workers maintain higher quality work than do American workers. A noticeable difference existed in the corrugated cardboard factories, as we have seen. The use of the spring device is an example of more attention paid to higher quality in Japan. Almost every Japanese worker has been trained to repair the machine when it breaks down. Only a few experts have the same training in America and Britain. This high level of technological mastery was probably acquired by schooling and on-the-job training. Professor Robert Cole of the University of Michigan, however, is strongly opposed to this view, which is to be stated later. If it turns out in our survey that a technological level in both countries is the same by comparison, then what makes the Japanese products superior? There should be some plausible reason if facilities and technological level for car production are approximately identical. What can it be? The answer is the very key to the secret of Japanese products.

TV PROGRAM, "IF JAPAN CAN..., WHY CAN'T WE?"

On July 28, 1980, a TV program originally produced in the United States was telecast in Japan after some re-editing. The title was "If Japan Can..., Why Can't We?"[6]

On the screen were scenes of various Japanese automobile factories. Comparisons disclosed why Japan had higher productivity and why her products excelled American products in quality. One example, QC (quality control) circle movement, was introduced in Japan. In another, Japan has 5,000 computerized robots, whereas America has only 200. This example was offered with the explanation that men should exercise their brains, not muscles. They go on to explain that Japanese workers participate in the overall enterprise and are on a high technological level. In the case of Donnelley Company in the United States, in which the Japanese method is incorporated, they manufacture products of high quality and their sales suddenly go up. Ther profits are shared by the employees who helped make quality better. Employees of Donnelley Company have truly realized that quality is absolute, and they have a high regard for Japanese technology. They assert as a fact that the absolute quality made them—employees of Donnelley Company—rich.

No defects of the Japanese system were brought out in the program. Our national pride was certainly tickled. Chairman Akio Morita of Sony Corporation made a comment, by way of explaining reasons for the facts presented in the program: "There is no difference in the quality of workers. The difference lies in the managerial system, how to draw upon expertise." Evidently, he is of the same opinion as Professor Cole of the University of Michigan.

Mr. Morita continues to say that Americans are great people as their history shows in their conquest of hardships. They have a whopping imagination, which allows accomplishment of creative projects. They are in no way inferior in quality to the Japanese. Give them a chance to try, and they will do it. He concludes that so far the chance has not been given to them. My opinion differs from Professor Cole's and Chairman Morita's on quality of labor. Japanese workers are far more efficient in mathematics and comprehension of principles and components of the machine. Their technological knowledge is much higher than that of American and British workers.

One indication is that Japanese workers possess technical skill to repair machine troubles. They are also capable of operating an adjacent work process in an operation. They will repair an electric drill if it is their own tool. Sufficient knowledge on a principle of the work process as well as on machines generates such capability. It was nourished in various on-the-job training programs, and this fundamental ability of comprehension was probably gained through education.

I am not of the opinion, of course, that one is inferior or superior to the other in human quality. But the level of technical skill, acquired through training or schooling, can be considered higher among the Japanese. Mr. Morita seems to lay stress on human quality when he emphasizes the ability of Americans. The ability I mean here is not the same as his, it seems.

Ability will be discussed later in reference to willingness to work. I want to confine the discussion here to the administrative system that Mr. Morita calls our attention to when he says, "Give them a chance to try, and they will do it. The chance has not been given to them." Professor Cole describes, too, that the difference between the two countries lies in their systems. I totally agree with him on this point. It is plain enough in the case of corrugate machine operators. All five or six operators are capable of tending machine troubles in Japan.

Let me cite an example of a cardboard feeder to the machine. Assistant operators are in charge of it in America and in Britain, because it does not take much skill. A fresh recruit can handle the job because no special training or practice is necessary. All he has to do is load a roll of cardboard 2 meters in diameter into the machine. When one roll is loaded and used up, the next roll has to be joined end-to-end without a break. This is the only part that requires a certain technique. The machine takes cardboard at the rate of 200 meters (219 yards) per minute at its fastest operating speed. The rate is lowered to 20 to 30 meters a minute at the time of joining. Correct timing is of vital importance during this phase. If the next roll is loaded too early, cardboard gets doubled and the machine stops. If the timing is late, cardboard will not be tri-folded because of the break. The next roll has to be timed so that only the slightest possible joint shows.

There is no marked difference in this skill of timing among Japanese, American, and British workers. They are all skillful as might be expected of specialists. The break in the operation because of missed timing is a problem.

In fact, it was Japanese blue-collar workers who contrived an automatic roll-loader which saves lots of trouble. It is called a splicer, meaning a joiner, as the word implies. This splicer, made in Japan, is in full use in America and England now. Until the splicer was made, the machine had to be stopped for the next roll to be loaded. The splicer eliminated this several minutes' delay.

Timely use of this splicer is important. The question is, what are the workers to do when they get out of timing? This actually happens in all countries. The machine does not come to a stop in Japan; whereas it does in America and England. They start it all over again.

But why? A difference of technical level. In the splicer, there is a roller for the cardboard to rotate into the machine smoothly. The cardboard rotates around the roller and into the machine. The workers in Japan, the moment they see that the machine might go out of timing, pull one end of the cardboard and connect it directly to the machine. This is what we do when we connect battery and engine directly in a car.

A splicer is a device to connect one end of the cardboard to the other. If the connection is likely to fail, one can do it manually, not using the splicer. If you forget a key to the car, direct connection to the engine is a solution. It is only possible when you are well acquainted with its structure.

"It is unbelievable! What surprised me most while visiting corrugated cardboard factories in America and England is that they stop the machine when the splicer does not work. Then, they scrupulously put the cardboard through the roller to start all over," production chief of K. Plant of R. Company in Japan spoke reminiscently.

Why do they stop the machine and start it all over again? It goes back to a difference in administrative systems. Production chief of K. Plant was surprised at their lack of technique, in a word. A decisive cause of it is that people in charge do not know what a splicer is used for. They also do not know how it is built. If they do, they tend naturally to switch to a manual operation.

I am not going to discuss here whether they have potential ability to understand the structure. In America and England, at least, they just operate the machine as they are trained. No instructions about its structure and application are given. Whether to train the men to understand the structure and function of the machine is a management and system problem. If the management expects an ad hoc measure out of them, they should give them a chance to learn the structure and function of the machine. They are not given that chance in America and England.

The invention of the splicer is an outcome of those instructions being given to workers in Japan. Since the splicer is their own invention, operation comes easy, and an applied action, the use of hands for a direct connection of cardboard without stopping the machine, came into practice.

Both Mr. Morita and Professor Cole contend that superior quality of Japanese products and high productivity are attributable to management ingenuity. To be more precise, we should say that it is a matter of management and the system that utilizes the full ability of workers. It is greatly questionable whether a change in management will bring about another Japan. There certainly is a successful case like the Tarrytown Plant of General Motors, for which Professor Cole is a consultant (to be discussed in more detail in chapter 5). But as American journalists agree, Tarrytown Plant is an exceptional phenomenon.

Why does management expect only what they order to be done out of workers? Why not let them think while they work? Most probably, it is because of a difference in the cultural foundation. A difference in management principles induces a difference. On the American and British side, job details are specified in so-called job descriptions, and on the Japanese side, the job details are left ambiguous, and workers are expected to perform a wide range of related jobs. QC circle movement was originally advocated by Dr. William E. Deming, an American. Dr. Deming, on a Japanese public TV program on July 28, 1980, talked on the issue and maintained that the reason for a successful introduction of QC circle in Japan and its unsuccessful introduction in America has much to do with differences in attitudes and ways of thinking.

A difference between the two countries pivoting around the splicer is a difference in the system of manpower utilization or willingness system. Meritocracy does not work well where workers accomplish only what they are told to do and only in the manner that they are instructed. Contriving, thinking, and striving are essential. The most important of all is not to set limits on work, like loading cardboard onto the splicer as one's limit. In the American system of willingness, a standard operation has been established, and nothing further has been anticipated. Achievement is limited to the standard. If they fail to reach the standard, they get a cut in their reward.

The same is not true in Japan. Take the case of QC circle. Everyone strives and competes to come up with a proposal for betterment. But they do not get a cut in wages because of a small number of proposals. Instead, one's effort is clearly seen in graphs put here and there in the factory. Japan utilizes a merit mark system, not a demerit mark system. The fundamental philosophy is that merits should know no bounds, just as the Japanese system of willingness presupposes. It has originated from a limitless, dispersing nature of work.

As stated before, technological and skill level is placed on the vertical axis in the comparative study of organizations in the United States and Japan. Comparison is being made according to the number of specialists involved. If so, standard ability alone does not make sense in this context of technological and skill level. A standard on a different basis has to be established. Just the ability to operate the splicer is not enough. What is needed to cope with the work along the assembly line is low technique and patterned skills. However, a clear distinction has to be made among those low levels of technique depending upon whether they have an ability for application. Weighing a standard operational skill level for the splicer in the balance is not equal to weighing real merits. A higher skill level or higher technological understanding by the workers in this sense accounts for the superior quality of Japanese cars, in a more important way.

THINKING BLUE-COLLAR WORKERS

Mr. Lou, a personnel manager of the main office, deeply concerns himself with a Japanese way of management. S. Company in Chicago for which he works exports electric tools to Japan. Quite a few businessmen in Japan must be making a bookcase or a fence on Sundays, using the tools made by S. Company.

When evening comes, Mr. Lou comes into contact as much as possible with the foremen. For instance:

"How was Lisa today? Was she doing all right?"

"Yes, she seemed to be all right."

"What do you mean by 'seemed'? Did you talk to Lisa, or didn't you?"

"I didn't talk to her. I just saw her a bit."

"What! You did not talk to her? Go to her right away and talk to her. Talk about anything you want. Let her know that the firm takes interest in her."

In America, the foreman is regarded as a cat's paw of the company, and people shun him and keep their distance from him. The old-time Japanese policeman might be its equivalent. "Hey, you there. You do this and that." Those will be his cliche. Mr. Lou has started his improvement plan with this point. And he framed a policy of talking about whatever you like with workers.

His biggest achievement is said to be that no union has been formed. He takes pride in it, too. Mr. Lou and I had a discussion on Japanese and American factories based on our experiences, comparing the two. Take an example of the spring device. What merits will a small device of spring bring about? A difference of $3,000 per person a year is our guess. High productivity in Japan is often attributed to long working hours, but this is not true. According to Mr. Lou's evaluation, it is because a Japanese worker produces $3,000 more than his American worker in a year.

Anyhow, Mr. Lou says that Japan is substantially a country with an ability system which is supported by meritocracy. Never does the seniority system get in the way of meritocracy.

A decisive difference between Mr. Lou's factory and a Japanese factory is whether employees have "freedom to think." If they are given freedom to think, ten people at $3,000 each will mean an extra $30,000 worth of productivity. There could be a miscalculation, but in a sense, a limitless productivity gain beyond our imagination may be hidden in the workers' minds.

Blue-collar workers in America, in general, are not given freedom to think. All they do is produce what they are ordered to produce in a prescribed manner. They are not free to alter the operation process or method arbitrarily. White-collar workers inclusive of foremen upward will attend to these affairs. It is clearly stated in the description of duties. Job descriptions for blue-collar workers make no mention of thinking whatsoever. It is made clear that "related duties" traditionally does not comprise thinking.

The American ability system means only performance of a job ordered or what is stated as a duty. They expect that division of labor, specialization, and minute differentiation of operation and regulation of operational speed in accordance with the conveyor belt would bring about high productivity. It is called "scientific management" by an American, F. W. Taylor.

Not only the operation around the conveyor belt but also all operations under supervision are maintained by the common philosophy. Execution of prescribed work yields no further productivity other than what is given. An American ability system can rightly be called, as it were, a demerit mark system. Our Mr. Wright must face the reality of reduced pay as a result of making junk. When it comes to white-collar workers, though, the picture changes completely. I shall discuss this matter elsewhere.

Mr. Lou maintains that thinking is part of a job in addition to the execution of prescribed work. He thinks that this is how the spring device evolved. This is what he calls a true ability system. Freedom to think and the right to think have to be provided with the ability system as the nucleus.

What troubles Mr. Lou goes deeper. Americans do not generally hold values that lead to the freedom to think or the right to think. Adoption of a suggestion system makes goof-offs who loaf on the job writing a suggestion, or who set their heart on writing a statement of reasons to the effect that the reward for suggestions is too small. It is not established as a system, and it comes down to the fact that their value system is different from that of the Japanese.

They loaf on the job and busy themselves writing a suggestion or a protest against a small reward for suggestions, because they presuppose that thinking is not part of their job. Extra work necessitates extra pay, and they think that a suggestion earns extra pay while their salary is fixed. This phenomenon will not take place if both thinking and work along the conveyor belt are included and systematized within the fixed pay. Mr. Lou is stuck here. "Man is a thinking reed." Taylor's Scientific Management made man a part of the machine. All he has to do is to be engaged in repetitive work while the switch is on. No need to think, nor is thinking allowed. What Mr. Lou asserts, therefore, is a liberation of man. Otherwise the ability system is dead. There is a limit to the ability of a machine, but man's ability is limitless. There is a possibility, and Japan has actually proved it.

But American management has eliminated freedom to think in work, and its elimination has taken root in the value system. Both American and British people had a big surprise at the fact that the spring device was contrived by the blue-collar workers in Japan. The Americans and British became aware of the catch phrase, "thinking blue-collars," which strikes us as neither fresh nor astounding.

HOW A NEW RECORD WAS BORN

Yakima Plant of W. Company is located in Yakima, Washington, which used to be an American Indian reservation.

"This probably is the most brilliant stuff in this plant," remarked the general manager as he pointed to a plaque, while I was visiting there. It was the pennant that showed the new record of corrugated cardboard production.

October 24, 1974, by J. Ellenberger
1,735,083 SQ feet
217,200 SQ feet per hour

Details revealed that Ellenberger produced about 50,000 SQ meters on October 24, 1974. The new record had been inscribed and honored permanently on the pennant. The inscription was engraved beautifully in the gray shield, and the pennant itself was patterned after the W. Company flag. It is radiantly displayed in a spot where it cannot escape notice. This must, doubtless, be a most prized possession of this factory. They say that the record cannot easily be broken.

It was October 9, 1978. On this day we encountered something which we will remember the rest of our lives. It was in Kawaguchi factory of R. Company in Japan. A new record of 72,372 SQ meters was established by Suzuki team, the first shift (from 7 A.M. to 3 P.M.) of the day. Our team was conducting a survey in the factory on that day. We had lunch of croquette and fried vegetables for 170 yen (70 cents) in the cafeteria of the factory, while the record was in progress.[7] It is likely that the members of the team had the same menu or noodles for 80 yen (33 cents), but nobody made us aware of their headway with the production then. They must have been on the stretch of "possible establishment of a new record." Later, they told us that they had been anticipating that there might be a turn of the tide by 3:00. We were informed of the news of a new record at the meeting which started at 3:30 P.M. The meeting was that of QC circles, and we intentionally chose October 9 as the day for our survey because we were informed that the QC meeting was to be held then.

The meeting impressed us as being somewhat unusual. We thought the meeting would start with repeated "Banzai! Banzai!" (Long live the Emperor!), since there had been a new record established, but it was really calm and quiet. It was not until the meeting had started that we learned the news. We gathered from the words, "A new record was established today," that it was not presented as any special event. The members seemed to have been suppressing any excitement. In spite of themselves, the suppression gave way to smiles on their faces. They could not completely conceal their feelings.

The incident could be a matter of paramount importance. In fact, they were busy analyzing what led to a new record. Several commendable actions could be referred to. Watchful eyes on the flow of the cardboard found the peeling off or breakage before it happened, which would induce an immediate emergency step to be taken and thus saved time. It was several days later, though, that they realized that attentiveness and close contact and cooperation with each other played the most important part. Every worker has to watch for a possible peeling off. When it is likely to happen, an instantaneous signal has to be sent to the machine chief in order to slow down the conveyor belt. Once the machine stops, some minutes are lost before it is switched on again. The machine has to be stopped when cardboard scraps are caught in its grooves, too. Before this happens, the machine should be slowed down and the scraps taken out. The machine has an overall length of 50 meters (slightly more than 150 feet). Attentiveness and cooperation of every worker is the key to establishing a new record.

The awareness of this nature was touched upon lightly. Chief Suzuki mentioned only once: "Everybody minded their business and did well." Their emphasis during the discussion was mainly on their good luck nevertheless. Other possible contributing factors were that most of the products were of the same sizes, the machine operation was smooth, and paper quality was good. The QC circle concluded, "Remind the supply section to pay extra attention to purchasing materials of good quality hereafter." Suzuki team surpasses Yakima Plant of W. Company by 40% in the record.

With the pennant of Ellenberger in front of us, we were reminiscent. Both achievements were made with machines of the same model during an identical time span.

BAFFLING STRATEGY BY MR. WRIGHT, A JUNKMAKER

The Suzuki and Ellenberger teams are Japanese and American aces. Their confrontation must be of great interest. They have something like the Olympic slogan in common: Higher, Faster, and More Beautifully.

Their ability must have been exerted in full. A challenge to a new record has to be *yaruki* beyond organization and reward. An establishment of a new record itself is of value, whatever pay they might receive. Reward is nothing but supplement. Confrontation of aces seems to fall in the dimension beyond seniority and ability systems.

But then, Suzuki team is not an ace with no other team to follow in Japan. It should be noted that a crowd of teams as powerful as the Suzuki team exists. Japan is unlike America at this point. America is quite thin in the number of good teams, so to speak. And at every level, it cannot be denied that American teams are not so powerful. It is shown in the comparison between the aces.

A major reason for this is the pressure the Japanese seniority system has on workers. Under a seniority system, pay and position go up, regardless of achievements. Loafing on the job might not be so noticeable. It is true that some white-collar workers rest on the seniority system. White-collar workers are entirely different in category, and

Japanese productivity goes down with them. Their sales are small, and supervisors with more than enough men under them are less productive than those in the United States, for all that. This tendency is strong among government workers. An essential element of their value is their awareness of qualification, not merit, among others.[8]

But those resting on the seniority system are the few exceptional cases. In the production scene, the fruit of one's labor clearly shows up. One cannot possibly loaf on the job, and a junk-making Mr. Wright will be obliged to leave the job before he gets fired. The Japanese seniority system stands on the premise that, at the least, workers' abilities are equal. If one is inferior in ability like Mr. Wright, he cannot be in the same boat, he is made to get out of it.

In many a case in Japan, a junkmaker like Mr. Wright is not left alone. They talk such a person into transferring to another section. He might turn into a watchman of the laboratory. The Japanese seniority system assumes, in the lower limits, an equality in ability and, in the upper limits, promotion by selection. People in general seem to interpret ability system as "competition among the highly capable" which the selection implies. In this sense, an ability system is pertinent to an elite class in America, but in its treatment of the lower limits, the Japanese seniority system will be closer to a merit system.

The following strategy against the personnel manager by a junkmaker, Mr. Wright, is suggestive of the very genuine nature of the American seniority system. Even the general staff of the army will be amazed by the strategy by supposedly unintelligent Mr. Wright. In the fall of 1979, his hourly wage was $5.92; his position: printer operator. Eight hours of work a day brought him about 10,000 yen a day, 200,000 yen a month if he worked twenty days a month. With occasional overtime, his average income came to about 250,000 yen (about $1,100) a month. In terms of work history, he has nineteen years in continuous service, and he is forty-seven years old. Three children out of four have grown up and left home, and he lives with his wife and a sixteen-year-old high school boy. He has been annoyed by the fact that he received two "written warnings" in the past year. A third warning will result in his dismissal from the company. Mr. Wright has been fighting with his back to the wall, so to speak. A Japanese, under such circumstances, will swear in his heart that never again will he produce junk. He could think of no other alternative. But Mr. Wright developed a totally different approach. His mind was set on misleading the personnel staff. He proposed to the production manager, "I want to be demoted to assistant operator."

His title is that of operator. If the title "assistant" is added to "operator," he loses 43 cents an hour. In eight hours he loses about 800 yen ($3.50). Besides the decrease in pay, scarcely any difference in the treatment is seen except for the fact that one's self-respect is injured. Being an assistant does not really mean that you assist a printer in his work. The printing job is still handled by one person. so the work stays the same. Another important factor is that he will be promoted by the seniority system in a year or two anyway. Whether he likes it or not, he will be an operator all over again. His hourly wage will be back to $5.92. Under conventional rights, the seniority system assures one of a raise in pay and a promotion even if one receives warnings.

Mr. Wright made beautiful use of this institutional defect. He himself proposed to be demoted because of his junk-making. That assertion at least makes sense.

Mr. Wright's tactic had the production manager tearing his hair out. Mr. Wright's proposal of his own demotion does make sense and cannot be turned down. Warnings have to be started over, though there is no precedent. The record of two warnings so far is to be cancelled. Demotion is a punishment any way you look at it. With the third warning, one is fired. After the second warning, one is demoted. It is a reasonable disciplinary measure in its own way. It certainly is a superb tactic by Mr. Wright. As long as the company adopts a seniority system, a vicious circle of warning-demotion-promotion will go on. To be frank, the company does not need Mr. Wright. They would rather discharge him. The problem is that if firing is repeated, the company loses the loyalty of workers toward management, thus workers become more and more unmanageable.

Mr. Wright's tactic is ingenious. He cunningly uses his brains. Why does he not make the best use of his brains in his work instead of in the confinement of management? That remained incomprehensible to our survey team.

What if Mr. Wright changed his workplace to Japan? He could not possibly stick to his post. In the corrugated cardboard factory, where they produce upon acceptance of orders, his shiftlessness will have to be covered by somebody else. Work is done as a team in Japan, and one team member may be obliged to work overtime, so that they all make the delivery date. Japanese companies have a reputation for keeping delivery dates as well as for maintaining high quality. A seniority system in Japan presupposes the same amount of merits. By staying in the position after proposing demotion, one will receive benefits while another members bears his burden. That situation would be unbearable. It is only a matter of the value system, whether one feels the mental burden or not. But Wright's art of self-protection will not succeed in Japan because of a merit system based on and supported by the value system. You may call it the principle of equality on a higher level. Thus, as a comparative study with America reveals, the

Japanese seniority system, with its characteristic merit system, works as a strong pressure at least on the production floor.

REVOLT OF NANCY

Nancy is nineteen years old. She works at a manufacturing plant of Y. Company near Liverpool. Top management of Y. Company tried an experiment. More efficiency is achieved when workers cooperate, rather than when each works on his own. Two persons will be able to carry what one person cannot. Nancy has joined a team of five members. This group method involves a risk, however. When merits are measured by group, not by individual, group members are liable to loaf on the job. This happens because responsibility of each individual is not made explicit. Details of the method by Y. Company are that productivity is measured as a set of five and that a 5% bonus will be given if production exceeds the old measure. They will each get a bonus if the new sum total of each member amounts to more than before. Nancy was included in this bonus system. The reasoning of the top management was as follows: Operation time will be shortened by each lending a helping hand to the other. Formerly, if an operation was delayed, the worker in the next step simply was idle while waiting, but when working in a team, workers should willingly help finish the delayed operation, hence a gain in the productivity.

The intention of the management up to this point was easily followed and well taken. By bringing a simple principle into operation, daydreaming during work will be a story of the past. Nobody raised an objection or expressed doubt on the side of management. Expectation swelled. Suppose Nancy gets a 5% bonus. She will be very happy. She will double her effort to break the record and to gain the second bonus. She will have to stop being a blabbermouth, sneaking time, and walking around. Everybody thought of it as an efficiency-breeding-efficiency system, not a mere dream. There was greater production, to be sure, for the first month than when the five had worked separately. Nancy and the rest were all smiles with a 5% bonus. Things proceeded as management had speculated. It will end the argument if one explains this by saying that their past production was much too low. But, at any rate, the system started rolling on toward efficiency-breeding-efficiency.

Sure enough, the second month broke the record of the previous month. Now it was the company executives' turn to be all smiles. They felt that what the Japanese call *yaruki* was aroused. Success was theirs if things kept rolling on and circulating in their favor. Even with a payment of a 5% bonus, they would make plentiful profits.

The third month was over, with the third 5% bonus. The Japanese way of working as a team seemed to have been welcomed here in Liverpool until an event took place one day. A customer claimed that the products were easy to break and sent them back. Since the application of the group method, five as a team, the whole set-up was arranged so that each member's share was easily discernible from the rest for the purpose of inventory control, besides a pool calculation of merits within the five. Cause for the claim was, therefore, easily traced. Products are tested for their strength. It is done manually after the machine automatically fabricates the goods. It was Nancy who performed the test to the claimed products. The test for strength requires little skill, just stretching with both hands. Either she had no luck or "heaven's vengeance is slow but sure," and the slack in Nancy's work was showing. Seemingly, Nancy busied herself chatting and cut corners. There was every reason to believe it, because all she had to do was give a pull to the goods, and she did not even do that.

There unfolded a typical scene where a group member's blunder puts the whole team into trouble. To their great regret, productivity showed a drastic drop because of those inferior goods, and naturally the 5% bonus was not repaid to them. The company notified the five of the nonpayment of bonus upon showing them their production total. Nancy held her tongue as a matter of course. She gave no excuse to the other four members. Self-examination of this kind is indispensable to a team, and this event might help establish the team system and make it solid. An interaction of this nature exists in Japan as far as I know.

The four did not keep quiet, though. Their counterattack was vehement. "We exerted our full ability and achieved more efficiency as we had pledged. We are entitled to a bonus." The executives pondered. They could not deny the fact that the four contributed to the productivity regardless of the outcome. Their efforts have to be admitted. Besides, Nancy has been blaming herself, and it will do her good in the future. You should not get other people into trouble when you work. It counts as essential if you want to make merits as a team, not just for yourself. You work for others too, so as not to inflict yourself upon them. That is the purpose of a team system.

The management gave the four 5% bonuses, with notes which read that the full exertion of their ability was appreciated and their continuous diligence hereafter is anticipated. The case was closed, it seemed. Much to everybody's surprise, Nancy had been far from being appeased. Nancy rose in revolt. "I am a nineteen-year-old girl. Physically, I am not so strong as a grown man. Isn't it a company's mistake to assign a job of strength tester to a physically inferior girl? I am entitled to a bonus if it is a reward for a full use of ability. I did my job within my range of physical strength."

This new development took the company by surprise. They, of course, turned down her request. It was on everybody's mind that Nancy was loafing on the day in question. They thought that she was just bluffing, because there was no proof. After she had her say, she would take back her request. They kept on turning up their noses at her.

Nancy persuaded the union leaders. They sided with her. It appeared that the case was going to be brought before the court. The issue had brought about a severe confrontation between labor and management.

At any rate, the merit method by team came to a deadlock on account of this incident. Management might be obliged to pay a bonus even in the absence of merit. Under the old system, where individual responsibility alone is pursued, the incident would be important enough that Nancy could be punished by a fine. It deserves a warning, at the very least.

The company concluded that it is unwise to stir up the confrontation between management and workers any more. They gave Nancy the 5% bonus and declared the team method invalid. A team of five is helpful in making merits. The lesson of this incident is that a system not backed by overall values is ineffective. The other four did not admit their responsibility for Nancy. Nancy, too, lacked the attitude that she was working for the other four. They all shared the value system of protecting an individual's profits by an individual. Another significant factor is that they had no awareness whatsoever of "working for the company at the same time." Some awareness of sharing profits was seen. All five of them gained bonuses regardless of overall production levels. In any case, a bonus is a worker's profit and the company's loss. The interests of employers and employees are set against each other.

A rising curve of profits cannot be hoped for unless members of the team hold the values that one works for the other four and each of the five works for the company. When quality of labor is questioned, some contend that there exists no great difference in individual skills between Japan and other countries. This may be a true statement, but how to get a person to give full swing to work is not a proposition to be worked out by management alone. Under a group system, a person exerts his ability, and it is the business of management to organize it into a corporation in some way. Adoption of a group system does not always prove successful, nevertheless. It is the values of workers that maintain the management system. It is their value system that works as a yardstick to decide labor of superior or inferior quality.

MULTIPLICATION IN TWO DIGITS

"Every time I ask him to check the inventory, he blunders. I am running out of patience," so griped the production manager abruptly.

"When I received a call from a customer, I told him to check the inventory, and he said there was just enough. I told the customer that we can make delivery today and hung up. We started loading, and then we found out we needed ten more."

We arranged a meeting with Brown, the stockman. We questioned him about his last mistake in calculation. This was his answer. "There sure was enough stock when I looked. It could be that somebody took them away." He made no comment to our next question, "You mean you were out of stock?" It was obvious that he did not want any downgrading. Later we watched his counting with interest. He was counting hundreds of stock items one by one. I would not be surprised if he came up with a different sum each time he did it, just the way a poor hand at the abacus does in Japan.[9] Most Japanese, even poor hands at abacus, will be able to tell the sum at first sight when there are 10 in a file, 11 in line, with a remainder of 2. I told him right away the sum of 112. He looked at me as if I were some sort of god. For him, multiplication in two digits was difficult, it is higher mathematics. This kind of calculation is not a difficult job for a Japanese, even if he did not go to senior high school. Management decided to give new job instructions to Brown. Just array the stock neatly lengthwise and crosswise and make a report of the number only in these terms.

There was a dispute over quality of labor. Is the quality of the Japanese superior or is it the same as Americans and the British? The dispute started when a big issue was made of Japanese exports of TV sets and cars to the United States and the European community. At any rate, Japanese goods have fewer breakdowns and are superior in quality in a variety of ways. It is because the quality of Japanese labor is good and that of the United States is not good. The production equipment is no different between the two countries except for the iron and steel industries. As to iron manufacturing, since the United States companies neglected investing in new equipment and old machines are still in operation, Japan outdoes them in excellence because of the processing equipment. However, we cannot but think of quality of labor when we dispute the quality of cars and TV sets.

Professor Robert Cole contended that America is never inferior in quality of labor.[10] Let us consider what he has to say. Japan ranks higher in the quality of cars, but Professor Cole does not think that technological know-how in the Japanese automotive industry itself exceeds that of the United States. But then, why are Japanese goods better in quality? One of the influential factors in quality of labor is a standard of education. Among semi-skilled workers in the assembly plant of GM, for instance, the number of high school graduates surged from 30% in 1960 to 67% in 1972. Quality of labor is on the upgrade. American workers' zeal for work, too, never compares unfavorably with that of Japan. Take for example the Tarrytown Plant of GM. In 1976, management started a group training program for workers, which contained a section on the systematic procedures for solving problems. As a consequence, workers began to occupy themselves eagerly in thinking out quite a few devices, and labor-management relations showed an apparent sign of improvement. Tarrytown Plant transformed from GM's worst assembly plant into one of its best. In short, America is not inferior in quality of labor to Japan.

What management puts priority on plays a key role here. American goods are inferior to Japanese goods, because Japanese management has put higher priority on quality than American management in the past several years. Japanese management took the lead in the direction of quality improvement, through strenuous emphasis on small groups of workers such as QC circles. On the other hand, not until recently has American management encouraged workers toward improvement of the quality of their own goods.

It is not that Japan has labor of better quality or that their goods excel those of America. The issue has nothing to do with the quality of labor. It is a matter of management policy. People have recently begun to get wind of this fact in America. Many companies are seriously directing their efforts toward betterment of product quality. Over a hundred companies have begun to introduce QC circles into management. We cannot tell whether these experiments will succeed or not at this stage, but undoubtedly American management has learned a new administrative method and is trying to introduce it.

Professor Cole concludes as follows: The misconception of the Japanese will incite arrogance and contempt over America. The trend will be detrimental to both countries which are interdependent economically and politically. Japanese tend to underestimate friends or foes by thinking of themselves as "number one."

The above is a summary of the arguments by Professor Cole. In addition, he included findings from a survey among workers in Detroit and Yokohama to justify his argument. His findings differ from ours. We might say that his analysis is rather optimistic. Professor Kenichi Odawara of Sophia University cites an instance of importance in opposition to the argument of Professor Cole.[11] He investigated the reason why the price of American cars doubles after they arrive in Japan, which the Americans say is incomprehensible. He points out that charges for labor ultimately double the price because American cars have to be disassembled and put together again in order to market them in Japan. Above all, Professor Odawara claims that quality of labor is to be questioned for this disassembling and rebuilding.

There is a trend in the American cities that affluent whites move out of the communities when poor blacks move in, making a clear distinction between the poor communities and the rich. Since education is dependent on finances of each community, it follows that the standard of education is lower in poor communities. And their quality of laborers falls behind that of rich communities. He also indicates that labor and management have opposing values. This can be seen by the fact that workers tend not to participate in production or quality improvement. It can also be seen in strikes, struggles for high wages, and in movements against introduction of new technology.

We cannot possibly discuss all the issues mentioned. Let us focus our attention on one of the points, quality of labor. It may be true that 67% of the American semi-skilled workers are high school graduates, as Professor Cole says, but their calculating ability seems to be lower than that of Japanese junior high school students. They fail to take charge of their own products. It is a very curious fact that about half of all senior high school students drop out in Chicago and near the Detroit area, where Professor Cole conducted his survey. It happens in Japan, too, that some students in senior high school are obliged to take basic math at a junior high school level. Nonetheless, most Japanese—of whom 94% are senior high school graduates—can multiply in two digits with ease. There evidently seems to exist a difference in quality of labor.

It seems as though quality of labor is not in itself a problem in the Tarrytown Plant, which Professor Cole mentioned. Suppose the quality of labor compares unfavorably, a system that utilizes the ability of workers is the key, as Professor Cole suggests. There is no question that such movements as QC circles involve worker participation, which Professor Cole strongly supports. But the fact remains that worker participation in the system is a success in Japan but not in America. What values workers hold over the relationship between the organization and its members will, in part, account for the reason why the system is a success in Japan and not so successful in America.

3

Foreman

ATTACKERS AND DEFENDERS

The word *foreman* can probably be defined as a person who is an on-the-job supervisor. He is indispensable for supervising operations. He is utterly dreaded by workers on the shop floor and can be unapproachable. But our observation on the shop floor in America and England makes us realize that the work cannot be performed without the foreman. The job simply does not proceed unless the foreman keeps watch on the workers. Wages symbolize the system of willingness in the sense of no work, no pay. Workers are not responsible, though, for the machine that is out of operation. An extreme case is when workers continue being paid after they jam a machine and take no notice of it. It is a principle, especially in England, that people get paid according to their qualifications. Workers can get paid in spite of loafing on the job unless they are on piece-rate jobs. Therefore, foremen are absolutely necessary. They watch out for loafers and cut their wages or even fire them. Foremen are on the front line of the company, acting as agents.

We came across a situation which made us well aware of how a foreman is received. We were having an interview with Harv, when Mr. Crosby, the foreman, opened the door and came in. Harv muttered, "Here comes a louse," wanting to be heard. Mr. Crosby, wearing a necktie, pretended not to hear him and seated himself in a nearby chair. The timing of Harv's comment was truly astonishing. He had known that the foreman would join us, and he had been quick-eyed enough to see him the moment he opened the door. He did not speak up just at that moment but waited until the foreman could hear him and muttered, "Here comes a louse." He did not say this to his face, and the foreman could do nothing but look the other way. He probably learned the knack of it through practice. "How would you like to go up to someone and say, 'I would like to go to the bathroom.' If the foreman doesn't like you, he'll make you hold it, just ignore you. Should I leave this job to go to the bathroom, I risk being fired."[1]

Now it was the foreman's turn to speak. With Mr. Crosby there was a sweeping change of tone. He says that his job is to make sure they do a good job and to push them ever harder. "I'll change my tour—so they can't tell every day I'm going to be in the same place at the same time. The worst thing I could do is set a pattern, where they'll always know where I'll be."[2]

Hearing both sides, we can see bitter antagonism between the two. It is beyond the foreman's powers, however, to fire workers. It is commonly the plant manager who is authorized to do that. The foreman uses evidence of offenses and gives out warnings. As a general rule, it is not until the third written warning that workers get dismissed.

It is an actual and realistic feeling by blue-collar workers in America and England that they are roughly handled by foremen, who are apparently the company's tools. If the Japanese management system were under discussion in America and England, the idea of a foreman would be in question. What role will a foreman have to play in an actual worker participation program? Many American managers and executives say that he should "suggest" and not "order." Many foremen say that workers never perform unless they are forced to. Some foremen say that they try to give gentle reminders or suggestions. The word *foreman* has a bad connotation, like "hey, you," or "boss." Therefore, firms interested in Japanese management have made the words *foreman* and *boss* obsolete, substituting *supervisor* (meaning the same as foreman, but sounding much softer).

It is now alleged, plausibly, that foremen give suggestions, not orders. For instance, some say, "Better use earplugs so you won't hurt your ears," and "Better put your tools away, so you won't have to look all over when you need them." It will be odd to regard all these suggestions as Japanese. A suggestion naturally has its limits when it is given to an already reluctant worker. What is the case in Japan? In some cases, an order is a necessity, and in others, a suggestion may be enough. The biggest difference between the two foremen is that one is a member of a team, the other is a foe.

There exists no equivalent of American or British foremen in Japan. There are those in command and those in subordinate positions, but both are members of a team. A commander in practice performs his own orders as well as he conveys them to his subordinates. He is "taking the lead" and "setting an example," if I may use an old expression. He fulfills a role of setting an example as a member of a team, which was probably born out of a belief in profit sharing.

The personnel manager of the main office of W. Company in America comments on this point, "If I put myself in an hourly worker's position, I would feel it ridiculous to work." Overtime pay for an hourly worker is fixed. No extra allowance is added for extra production. But managers and foremen of the plant get bigger bonuses for higher production. Hard work does not pay off for hourly workers, only for executives. In other words, workers work for the profits of foremen and managers. What an hourly worker says stands to reason, to be sure, if we compare their pay arrangements: "They [executives] get prosperous by shouting at us. And the more they shout, the more bonuses they get."

BIG BET OF A HARVARD-GRADUATE MANAGER

The following scenario took place at O. Factory of W. Company in America. We had a conversation with Mr. H., a young graduate of Harvard Business School. He took his post here as plant manager with new ideas on management in his mind. Up until then, the factory had been in a state of disorder. It actually happened that repeated firings had replaced almost all workers in one year. "Firing was an everyday occurrence. There were so many jobless people that our waiting list was always full," says Mr. H. Just a slight loafing was good enough reason for firing, and recruiting was easy. This was repeated time and again.

O. Factory was not alone in this sequence of firing and recruiting. Our qualitative pursuit of this case must offer something comparable for Japanese management. Successive firing is in direct contrast with permanent employment, which in turn might give us some supporting ideas for permanent employment as an alternative. An analysis might give us a better feel for the relationship between supervisors and subordinates.

The former plant manager of O. Factory had convictions, which represented a mode of managerial thinking in America at the time: (1) The average human being has an inherent dislike of work and will avoid it if he can; (2) Most people must be coerced, controlled, directed, threatened with punishment to get them to put forth adequate effort. . . . [3] Foremen will be in great demand under these convictions. A foreman, a superior, is there in order to coerce, control, direct, or threaten "lazybones" with punishment. Behind his power is a daily threat of firing.

In Japan we do not presuppose people to be "lazybones," at least not until the recent younger generation, whom we will exclude from this discussion. We have very little need for "control," "direction," and "punishment." Accordingly, we are not in need of superiors in charge of "lazybones." What do we have supervisors for, then? According to organizational principles, a supervisor is a conveyer of orders, which was touched upon before. A Japanese supervisor off-duty is nothing more than a worker on the same line as the rest of the workers. He does not walk around and keep watch on the workers, but works together with them, except that he substantially leads while working. His long experience makes him stand out from the rest in ability. He is an authorized commander and punisher from the standpoint of organizational structure, but he is a family leader in function.

The situation does not call for him to be an authorized commander and disciplinarian, and he probably has a totally different outlook on employees in contrast with his American counterpart. Here are some examples of that philosophy:

1. The expenditure of physical and mental effort in work is as natural as play or rest.

2. External control and the threat of punishment are not the only means for bringing about effort for organizational objectives. Man will exercise self-direction and self-control in the service of objectives to which he is committed.

3. Commitment to objectives is a function of the rewards associated with their achievement.

4. The averge human being learns, under proper conditions, not only to accept but seek responsibility.

Douglas McGregor called the idea Theory X: "if left alone, people tend to be idle." That which assumes " 'diligence' as natural in man," he called Theory Y.[4] To be sure, "Commitment to objectives is a function of rewards" is somewhat unfamiliar to us. But this reward corresponds to "permanent stability" in Japan and will have more influence than bonuses in America. Indications such as "company going into bankruptcy," "likeliness of compulsory retirement,"[5] and "likeliness of demotion" are all the more pressing. McGregor's Theory Y is quite relevant to Japan in that close scrutiny by foremen is not necessary. With antagonism between foremen and hourly workers in front of us, it seems that Theory Y will remain a theory and will be impossible to put into practice. Application of Theory Y was only remotely possible at O. Factory of W. Company where workers were repeatedly fired. Foremen are not even required if workers work voluntarily and take on responsibility themselves. Mr. H., the Harvard graduate, eliminated foremen immediately after he assumed his position. It was quite a big bet. How on earth did it turn out?

It turned out to be a big success. Workers of the plant did work without foremen. Mr. H.'s faith or McGregor's Theory Y was a winner. Firing hardly takes place anymore. There was a jump of 30% in productivity in comparison to that of the former manager. Workers transformed into cheerful and vivacious beings.

America is now giving serious thought to introducing Japanese management techniques. A change in attitude by foremen is a concrete example of it. Some factories, such as O. Factory of W. Company, discontinued them completely. In others, they remain in power, but a total change in attitude is seen. They exchange greetings and converse with workers like friends, without expressing "order" and "punishment." They explain that it is because they "trust" workers.

INSIDE STORY OF THE BET

The manager of O. Factory of W. Company, who has faith in his workers, established a good reputation for practicing new ideas of management. Let us first listen to his account. He first surprised us by saying that he does not suspect an absentee to be an idler.

"How many are absent today?"

"Two."

"What is their reason for absence?"

"I don't know. In fact, I don't have to know."

"They might be playing hooky. Why not ask the reason?"

"My only concern is a smooth production in the factory for today. No concern whatsoever in their reason for absence."

"If you find out that they are just playing hooky, you can ask them to come to work. You can boost the production, can't you?"

"Well, in order to find out whether they are playing hooky or not, a medical certificate by a doctor will make a good proof. But then, I cannot trust it 100 percent. I have to look into the facts and see whether the certificate is genuine. I know better than wasting time this way. When you are absent, no pay. That's it. This is not a school to teach morals, to start with."

"If they are really suffering from sickness, is it not your responsibility as a manager to introduce doctors or visit sick persons?"

"A factory is not an institution for social security. I do not give a damn about their reasons for absence, as I told you before. Production won't be higher even if I go and see them. No work, no pay. It's the same thing whether you are playing hooky or sick. You simply lose a job if your absence amounts to more than wage loss. It is a waste of time to poke and pry the reason for absence."

Our conversation with Mr. H. covered an essential part of "human trust," and it seems to reflect a cultural difference between America and Japan as it is. What is the substance of trust when a supervisor says he trusts his subordinates? How is it alike or different from Japan? Mr. H. does not think of the men in the factory as moral beings. The Japanese tend to make a distinction between morally good and morally bad employees. If you admit that a worker is a moral being, then his reason for absence has to be questioned. If you admit that he is merely a producer, you do not care whether he is morally good or bad. You only question the outcome, whether he boosted production (and its appraisal looms large in your mind). If you think that he is a moral being, reason more than outcome is emphasized. Outcome is only a consequential reflection of being moral. Appraising the outcome, for that reason, becomes secondary, certainly not indispensable as a condition.

Mr. H. abolished foremen. Instead, he put individualized production data into the computer. One glance could determine whether production went up, down, or stayed the same. Suppose production is low, you do not question whether it results from negligence or poor health. In Mr. H.'s words, it is a waste of time to poke and pry. He also adds that the factory is not a classroom for teaching morals. Computers are exquisite foremen, quite unsurpassed. Regrettably, computers do not output feelings or personal morality. That might explain why hardly any companies in Japan put data of individual achievement into computers. Yet, Mr. H. does not say that his method is based on human distrust. Hard work shows itself truthfully in the computer (and that quite fairly and accurately). Unlike foremen in the past, the computer is not suspicious, says he. As proof, he mentioned the no-inspection system. He had abolished product examiners as well as foremen. He made a big point of this, saying that it is nothing less than trust.

Under this no-inspection system, products whose quality would not pass through inspection are forwarded to users anyway. To be sure, it is a feat of systematization which is not possible without trust in workers. Formerly, an examiner used to do a one-by-one quality inspection. Since examiners too had been sorted into the group of "lazybones," foremen to watch over them were absolutely necessary. On one occasion the foreman was not careful enough, and an enormous amount of inferior goods was passed to a customer, who in turn fined the company.

Inspection of goods is no longer possible with the abolition of the supervisor, foreman. It certainly is meaningless to continue to have a good-for-nothing examiner, a white elephant. Like Mr. H., if you accept McGregor's Theory Y which holds that "people work voluntarily and assume responsibility" as true, there is no use for foremen and examiners. Hence, he abolished the inspection system.

It appears to be nothing else but trust in men, but this does not settle the problem. What if the user returns the goods because of their inferior quality? Whatever trust he has in workers, is there not always a chance of producing defective goods? There is even a chance of the company going under on account of making so much junk. Overall, it seemed to be a risky bet.

But Mr. H. was clever enough to have a scheme set up to prevent a bankruptcy. Mr. H. certainly trusts workers, and his trust implies that workers "seek responsibility," not that workers take care "not to make junk!" It is not the trust that they never produce junk.

He had assigned responsible persons for each product. Thus, using the computer, he can easily and instantly locate the person in charge when goods are returned. The individual in question deservedly and personally assumes responsibility for making reparation for damages. Even in case of remaking, the individual is held responsible for the cost. There is trust for sure because the responsibility is placed on an individual person.

His trust had left some space for the computer, so to speak. His scheme is "premised on doubt in advance." It had the look of a risky bet, but it is so contrived that an individual runs his own risk. It is not a wildly risky arrangement. In Mr. H.'s words, the scheme presupposes responsibility—namely, the system has started with the trust that workers "seek responsibility." He never says that his distrust leads him to link the workers directly with the computer so that he can trace whose responsibility it is. In our eyes, his distrust and suspicion that workers may produce junk resulted in a scheme to find out who was liable.[6]

The underlying difference can be explained as follows: From a viewpoint of American culture, an individual is eager to avoid responsibility. Hence, it is an action well worth respect to assume responsibility and call it trust. From a viewpoint of Japanese culture, it is only natural to assume responsibility; one never dodges it. It is nothing as highfalutin as trust, rather, and "not to produce junk" is natural. We "trust" only that fine goods will be produced. The issue here is whether to install a computer in place of a foreman.

EVEN THE GREAT BUDDHA FORGIVES ONLY THREE TIMES[7]

One of the subjects in our interviewing happened to be a nurse. She asked us to come to the doctor's office because she had patients to look after. Nancy, a Spanish beauty in a white robe, was witty enough to hang her own portrait on the wall with the words "charming nurse" on it. It has created a relaxing atmosphere in the office, just as she intended.

With the Japanese-made sphygmomanometer in use, she answered our questions. After she was through with general questions, she gave us an account of various patients.

We sometimes get drunks in the morning. When they are bad, they are too much for me to handle. I call the police and hand over real wild ones to them.

They rage about and make quite a scene. They are so hard to handle. I let mild ones rest here for a while, but I don't know if they get sober enough to work. If bosses decide that some cannot stay on the job, they call up their families and send them home.

In case of women? Well, too much drinking is fairly rare. Most of their cases are overdoses of tranquilizers. They are dotty on their legs, so I can easily tell. We see one or two tranquilizer addicts a month, but quite a few drug addicts, though.

We could not let it pass. Drunks in the factory! Theirs is a manufacturer of electric appliances. We could not put drunks and electric appliances together. What is a foreman's reaction to it? What does he have to say about it? We were quite baffled by what he said:

A factory is not an executive organ of law or morality. The police will take care of violations of law, if there are any. If behaviors are against moral standard, well then, church or school should take care of it. A factory is a place to manufacture goods. How can management possibly tell workers not to take drugs or not to drink?

Do not drink, do not take drugs, give your kids a good education, do not quarrel with your spouse, go straight home, do not drink or play mah-jongg on the way, do not sit in front of the TV far into the night, get a good night's sleep, and take good care of yourself and so on. It will be odd for company executives to admonish workers for such behaviors, when you come to think of it.

It would not be too odd, though, to tell them not to drink before or during work even though you cannot ask them never to drink at all. Some might carry their liquor well and argue that they are perfectly sober and can do a good job. Then, you cannot argue back and tell them to refrain from such drinking as it will have a bad effect on work. Most probably, the effects have to be defined, in this case, such as normal judgment or steadiness on their feet, only to mention a few. Definition of the effect and its standard being fixed, we will have to discuss who is to judge and in what way. It might turn out to be a delicate problem.

There is a coherent conception of a good worker throughout American managers: If he is a failure as a worker, no job, that's it. Results tell whether one is a good worker or not. Some are heavy drinkers, some are not. Some even work better, the drunker they are. Results are everything. It is characteristic of American management to judge by result only. In case of absence, for instance, it is the fact of absence only that matters, as we saw previously. There is never a question of reason, such as sickness, a community meeting, or even making more money at another company for a day, which is sometimes the case in America.

I am talking generally, but it is not always the majority among American companies that judge by result only, never asking reason at all. Rather, this management philosophy is observed in well-organized companies with no familial elements in them. In addition, judging by result only is not possible until individual amount of work or quality are entered into the computer. You might say that this method goes along with computerization. Willingness is judged by computer results.

European management may be classified as "reason-ism." Europeans make much of "why" the result was brought about. Japanese management, on the other hand, makes much of the process as well as the result. A little intoxication in the workplace is good enough reason for a disciplinary measure in Japan, regardless of results. Work is a place for moral training, a classroom for ethics. Plenty of instructions like "Don't . . . without permission" are observed there.

The drunks under the care of the nurse, Nancy, will not get a warning just for being intoxicated in the Chicago plant of S. Company. They fire workers when their productivity falls under 85% of norm. It is very likely that drunks will produce under 85%. The warning by reason of drunkenness and that of low productivity reach, as the foreman in S. Company says, the same result. As the computer never lies about the result of work, it might even facilitate the firing. There will be no bandying of words, like "Yes, you were drunk" and "No, I wasn't," or there will be no use of a breathalayzer, which is all very troublesome.

Warning, by the way, is a rigid procedure of firing. As a general rule, an oral warning is given first, and only if three written warnings follow is one fired. A look at the form in figure 4 will tell you the rigidity of the procedure.

Department and name of the warned, action taken, and its reason are to be filled out on the form: Violation of Company Policy. A closer look will tell you that the original goes to the shop steward, a duplicate to personnel, and a triplicate to the foreman. The fact that the original goes to a union representative will impart to you in full its weight. Only a foreman need sign his name, but in practice, the violator and shop steward usually sign too. After three of these warnings, one loses a job.

The warning has an important part to play in a system of willingness to work in America and England. In fact, whether this system exists or not makes a critical difference as we make a comparative study with Japan. No written warning exists in Japan. Strictly speaking, though, there exists punishment by way of caution or no raise in pay for one year. Taking the case of a government office, they punish officers whom they have never seen for embezzling official money. There is no warning system in the actual workplace of the factory, at least.

It occasionally happens in America and England that one gets a

Figure 4. Warning Form: Violation of Company Policy

```
┌─────────────────────────────────────────────────────────────────────┐
│  ORIGINAL TO SHOP STEWARD                                             │
│  DUPLICATE TO PERSONNEL          VIOLATION OF COMPANY POLICY          │
│  TRIPLICATE TO FOREMAN                                                │
│                                                                       │
│                                     Date..................................        │
│                                                                       │
│  Dept.................... Name................. Clock No.................   │
│                                                                       │
│  Action taken: .....................................................................  │
│                                                                       │
│  ..................................................................................... │
│                                                                       │
│  Reason: ..........................................................................  │
│                                                                       │
│  ..................................................................................... │
│                                                                       │
│  ...................................................................... Foreman    │
│                                                                       │
└─────────────────────────────────────────────────────────────────────┘
```

warning because of absence without notice. Absence without notice itself rarely takes place in Japan, and if it does, there is some compelling reason, because it is a country of reason-ism. Yet, it is an undeniable fact that some will be under the care of the police at its drunk-protection center and absent themselves the whole day, and some will come late to work. Whatever plausible excuses may be given, what is doubtful is doubtful, and absentees will be placed on the "blacklist" of the manager after two or three absences instead of getting warnings. "Threat to be on the blacklist" is more efficacious than warning. "Tardiness 1" will be entered in the personal record when they are late, besides the threat to be on the blacklist, which has a strong effect. The Japanese system uses the threat to be on the blacklist in place of warnings.

4

Japanese Companies

A MISTAKE BY MR. BERT, AN EXCUSE-MAKER

> "You are always behind time. Can't you come back a bit earlier
> to work?"
> "It's not my fault. You installed the machine quite a distance
> away, that's why. Why don't you move the machine closer to the
> rest quarters? That's where I am. That is, if you want me to start
> earlier."

This was a conversation between a foreman and Mr. Bert, an hourly
worker at Y. Company in England. The two talk back and forth once
in a while, because Mr. Bert does not turn on his machine early enough,
obviously lowering his productivity. The foreman does not always ignore it, and Mr. Bert is sharply reprimanded.

One day Mr. Bert happened not to come back to work until almost
an hour later than he was supposed to after tea time. He explained
that he had encountered a traffic accident on the way from the nearby
pub, so it was not his fault. This excuse proved foolish, since the foreman easily found out that this story was false; there was no accident.
He made up such an easily traceable excuse that he was placed in an
embarrassing situation, received his third warning, and lost his job.
The union leader who witnessed all of this had no basis for arguing
on Mr. Bert's behalf.

So Mr. Bert himself argued against his firing. Later the case was
tried in the circuit court. The company won the case without question,
but Mr. Bert appealed to a higher court. Interestingly enough, he had
worked and received pay for several weeks before the trial as if nothing
was the matter. Very rarely (only under special circumstances) in Japan does the defendant get paid while on trial. We put this question
to the foreman: "Is Mr. Bert more militant than the ordinary person,
or has he more nerve, or is he thick-skinned?"

"He has a lot of nerve, yes, more than usual, maybe, but it is quite ordinary to continue with one's work while a case is on trial. It is not an awkward situation and his co-workers do not mind it at all."

In the meantime, he absented himself without notice for three days. He made an abrupt appearance on the fourth day and asked for the rest of his pay. Now it appeared that the chances were nine out of ten that he would lose his case.

"You admit that you were absent without notice?"

"Yes."

"You put your signature here. What was the matter with you? Why were you absent for three days without letting us know?"

"I guess I don't have to tell you. It's a private matter."

Since Mrs. Bert was working in the same factory, it seemed appropriate to consult her. She professed that she had nothing to do with her husband's case, being an entirely different person. The company totally agreed with her and so did her fellow workers. It was disclosed, however, in private, that Mr. Bert had been in police custody for three days for wife-beating.

The trial revealed that he had been fired twice from other companies for identical reasons. We asked the personnel manager about this point. He strongly defended himself, feeling he was being reproached for his poor hiring practices. "You may be right," he said, "I am responsible for having hired such a person. Think of my situation realistically, though. I spend three hours interviewing job applicants every day. Some tell lies as though they are truths. I can't possibly look into each statement. I'm behind in hiring as it is. I have to hire several men every single day. People quit every day, you see."

This frequency of replacing workers (in England) would be most unlikely in Japan. Rumor has it that Mr. Bert got a driving job at another company. There is a high probability that the other company also employed him without spending ample time on recruiting. Mr. Bert is a successful "migratory worker."

It is rather unusual for a worker to work for one company all of his life. The immediate future seems to be the limit of management's goals for its employees. To be beneficial to workers, the companies' goals must be longer range. One cannot blame only workers, poor management policies also produce migrant workers.

Yaruki, willingness to work, is not induced unless a company and its employees have common interests that are promoted only over a long association. Consistent movement of employees does not allow long-range distribution of assets. If the company depends upon short employment periods, then only temporary needs can be satisfied. We cannot forget this aspect of time when viewing the characteristics of Japanese companies, which underlie *yaruki*.

WHAT IS ON THE MINDS OF ABSENTEES?

The turnover (job changing) rate is 30% a year in S. Company in America and 60% a year in Y. Company in England. With 60% of employees walking in or out of a company during a year, a company of one hundred employees averages about five people quitting every month. This obligates interviewing and reviewing the resumes of twenty or thirty applicants to fill those vacancies each month. The personnel department is thus kept busy all year round; whereas in Japan it is busy one time in a year doing all hiring.[1] Personnel managers in both America and England often grumble that they are "damned" busy. Unlike in Japan, though, they are seldom kept occupied ranking workers for promotion or shuffling personnel. In all likelihood, Japanese personnel managers will say that they are even busier than the Americans or English, but with entirely different problems. Shifting of workers to different teams, isolating troublemakers, promoting some without antagonizing others, and maintaining *yaruki* are a few of the Japanese personnel manager's concerns. Rarely is there time to consider these inner workings in America and England.

Job specifications of a personnel department reveal not only the employment structure of a nation but also cultural differences. So a cross-cultural comparison of personnel managers may be revealing. Mr. F., personnel manager of Y. Company in England, told us that he spends considerable time hiring and firing.

It is also as important to analyze those who change jobs as it is to analyze personnel departments. Mr. F. and I ran into Frank Dole during a late lunch we had at a nearby pub. Mr. Dole, twenty-four years old, has a word that is not listed in the dictionary tattooed on his arm. He is the provider for his wife and son.

Mr. F. and Frank were surprised at seeing each other, but fondly shook hands. It was their first encounter since Frank changed jobs two months ago. He had worked in the factory under Mr. F. for six years. Under similar circumstances in Japan, they would probably have felt awkward and pretended not to recognize each other. But not in England. They accepted that people change jobs frequently. Their conversation went as follows:

"Where do you work now?"

"Driving a truck at A. Company."

"How much do you get?"

"Seventy-one pounds a week."

"Only that much? We paid you £85, didn't we? How come you took that job?"

"Eighty five included overtime on Saturday. Otherwise, it was only £56. I get over £90 at this place if I work on Sunday. It really pays well. You see, I only work four hours to get £71."

"£71 in four hours? That's super-duper. How does that work out?"

"Well, I work early morning hours, 5 A.M. to 9 A.M."

"That's rather tough, isn't it? No wonder you get £71. I still think that we treated you better."

"I prefer this job."

His hours explained why he could have some beer in the pub at two in the afternoon. To Frank it was evening, since he quits work at nine in the morning. But scarcely any other soul is seen in the pub at 2 P.M. He had been drinking all morning until we joined him. He said his reason for the job change was better working conditions, but I was confused by what he meant.

Here is his explanation. He goes home once work is over. Then he usually goes to the pub to drink. He has no companion to chat with in the pub; he is always alone. After he is comfortably drunk, he goes home and goes to bed. He works four hours a day and spends the rest drinking and sleeping. He likes to idle away time, and he was day-dreaming about buying a new car when we met him. I was very interested in what he thought of his job change. He said, "I am amazed at myself that I worked for Y. Company for six long years. My present job pays well, but I will take up another job if I get sick of drinking and sleeping."

His concern for the company is limited to working hours and pay. He is not concerned with friends, welfare, or relative complexity of and interest in the job. Mr. F. described Frank as an average British worker. We learned that Frank did take his work seriously and has high technical skill. These qualities had speeded his promotion faster than the average at Y. Company. If he had stayed with Y. Company one more month, he would have been promoted and given a pay raise of one pound a week.

Frank was alone in the pub when we joined him. The chairs were placed on tables for cleaning and preparation for further business. Frank was sitting with his arms folded, his mug of beer in front of him, looking friendless and lonely, in my opinion. He said he was fond of drinking by himself and passing the time in idleness. He changed his job when his promotion was just ahead of him, and he is thinking of changing to another job when he is tired of this one. He has no intention whatsoever of depending on his company. His only concerns

Figure 5. American Workers Think About Wages When Not at Work

"What was on your mind when you were absent from the company (wages, supervisors, co-workers, job, subordinates, family)?"

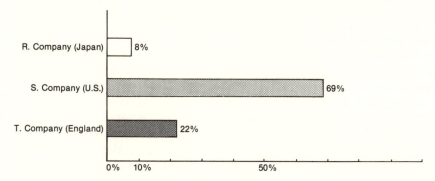

about his company are his hourly wages and, in the case of his new job, the shift.

What would prompt a change in his behavior? He might be conscious of "knocking off work," but will have no consciousness of being "absent from the company." For him no work simply means no pay. His absence might incur inconveniences to the customers of the company; the company might go bankrupt because of poor business; he will not see his co-workers; or he might inconvenience his co-workers (since they do not work as a team, this may be a lesser problem); thus, he might be on the blacklist. His family, especially his wife, might nag at him, or he might be self-conscious about his laziness. (People born in the first decade of Showa might be the last generation in this respect in Japan.) All these are matters of no great significance to Frank.

"What was on your mind when you were absent from the company?" We asked this question in terms of the following six categories: wages, supervisors, co-workers, job, subordinates, and family. Figure 5 shows the percentage of employees indicating "wages" in three different companies:[2]

Figures of "considerably" and "slightly" put together were 8% for R. Company in Japan, 69% for S. Company in America, and 22% for T. Company in England. There is quite a discrepancy among the three countries. This quantitative difference about being absent and wages may account for Frank's attitude.

A general overview on the inquired six items follows: What distinguishes the Japanese is that "work" and "human relationships" are on their minds when they are away from work. Human relationships among supervisors, co-workers, and subordinates imply an existence of "community." It contrasts in such a striking way with America and England that "wages" are overshadowed. What distinguished Americans were the categories "supervisors," "wages," and "family." It is likely that family, especially wives, nag at husbands if they do not bring back wages. Supervisors in America, unlike in Japan, care little about co-workers and subordinates. There is no sense of "community." What distinguished the British were "wages" and "supervisors." Unlike Americans, very few mention "family."

Americans seem to be under pressure from wives. The survey here does not clarify the reason. One opinion was that American women possess particularly great power, but this is only speculation.

The way I see it, Frank Dole, a silent beer drinker in the English pub, personifies English workers. He values no particular company; any company that offers work and wages will do. Far from having strong emotional ties with the company, he finds that companies in general are trying to cut his wages one way or another.

MISS S.'S FIANCÉ

After work at M. Electric Company, Osaka, Japan, QC circle groups of twos and threes were discussing the day's problems. One all-female group out of the twenty attracted my attention. Most of the groups were analyzing the cause of some defective products or the reason for an assembly line stoppage, but not this women's team. They were discussing more womanly matters: "How about a mirror? Flowers are more expensive than you think, you know." "An album may be just the thing."

The choice of a gift for Miss S., soon to be married, was their subject. They have decided that the value of the gift should be 3,000 yen (about $13), and Miss S., the recipient of the gift, included in the discussion, was also expressing her wishes. We had a chance to talk to Miss S.:

"Is your bridegroom-to-be in the same company?"

"He works as an engineer in the next building."

"Are you going to continue work after marriage?"

"No, I'm going to quit. I have saved money through company deposits, so I'm not too worried."

"How about housing?"

"He lives in the company dorm,[3] so we'll rent an apartment for the time being and will buy a house one of these days."

"You need a fortune to buy a house, don't you?"

"I know, but he says that we can afford one. He has been saving for the house through the company, he says."

"Can you tell me more about this saving system?"

"I don't know the details, but he has been saving since he entered this company. The company is responsible for the system, so I don't see any reason why we can't buy one."

Miss S. has security via the reserve fund for married life and housing. She has no misgivings whatsoever about her and her husband's future. Listening to her, I have keenly realized that she was actually marrying M. Electric Company.

Professor Robert Cole explains Miss S.'s situation which is commonly seen among Japanese as "dependency."[4] Miss S. is dependent on the company. If M. Electric Company goes bankrupt, her life will be ruined. Her fiancé's attainment of his objectives coincides with those of the company. Organizational prosperity and employee's prosperity are identical.

It is essential for employees to internalize the organizational objective in order for them to participate in the real sense. Miss S. and her fiancé have firmly accepted the company objectives as their own. It seems that internalization of organizational objectives and *yaruki*, willingness to work, go hand in hand. The goals of the organization will not be internalized if the company is expected to do nothing more than pay wages, as we saw in the case of Frank Dole.

Acquisition of wages is but one factor in human life. You have to be deeply committed in a variety of ways to the organization in order for your life in all aspects to be wedded to it. M. Electric Company is not the only organization that pays wages. Frank Dole has a wide choice. It could be Y. Company or any other express company.

For Miss S. and her fiancé, their attachment to the company is quite diversified; receiving wages is only one element. The company exerts influence on their retirement. Reserve funds for married life and housing act like an insurance policy. Relations with co-workers are central to their way of life. Babies can be delivered at bargain prices in the company-affiliated hospital. Supervisors may intervene in marital crises acting as counselor or go-between. Even miscellaneous daily necessities can be bought cheaply at company facilities.

A relationship based on wages only is a safe haven, according to Professor Cole, but it has no principal function in life. Americans are "dependent" on the company organization, but it is only a "partial dependence," as McGregor says. The more dependence that the company can generate makes the company less substitutable. But in the case of "partial dependence" the company is very substitutable. This substitutability is a peak difference between Japan, the United States, and England. The relationship of a Japanese employee with his company bears some resemblance to that of parent and child. A parent cannot be substituted for another just because he is no good, just as a child cannot choose parents. This forms a unique relationship: They sail in the same boat whether the company is going bankrupt or prospering, all due to "total dependency."

From a macroperspective, Japanese *yaruki* stems from this participatory spirit. Participation of this magnitude is not possible without the premise of a whole-personality linkage to the company. The whole-personality linkage is a reality in Japan, as Professor Cole says, because the company and its employees are linked at all levels.

But all-out dependence on the company is not valued in America. A total dependency of this nature is seen as a negative element, even as humiliation in some cases. When there is total dependence, one might be obliged to submit tamely to unreasonable demands. The all-out dependence must be promised on the goodwill of the other party (employer), or a worker will be placed almost in slavery. In case of too much dependence, a worker puts himself in a position where he cannot expect his rights to be respected. Americans reject the idea of the whole personality being engaged in an employment relationship. For them, every person is unique in that a person is not completely replaceable by another, and they insist that they keep the "right to choose."

It could be said that the Japanese *yaruki* is a product of the system that has cast away the "right of choice." M. Electric Company was a chance place of employment for Miss S. It was also chance that she met her fiancé there. Once the die was cast, she just stuck to it to the end. If she had chosen to, at any point, she could have started over, but she accepts things as her fate to be thus situated, not like Americans. Miss S. has not been conscious of it, but it is firmly fixed in her mind that neither her company nor her husband can be substituted for another.

Employees can be productive but replaceable tools for any company. Japanese history shows, though, that management did not exercise the privilege of substituting. During times of recession, executives and stockholders voluntarily took cuts and managed frugally, thus avoiding the dismissal of workers. The implication is that the company, management, and workers all share the same fate.

JAPANESE ARE RACE HORSES IN THE STABLE!

"The West is short and high, the East is long and low." This philosophical statement was said by Robertson at a discussion meeting at the factory of T. Company, near Cambridge, England. What he meant was that they work short hours and get high wages in Western European countries; whereas they work long hours and get low wages in the Orient. He was vague in his wording and said "the Orient," not "Japan," sounding all the more philosophical.

Robertson is forty-eight years old, a second-class operator with seventeen years of continuous service. His daily wage is about eight pounds ($18). In a month, with his usual overtime, he makes a little over $400. The West was not so high! His view of Japanese wages represents that of an average Englishman. He was very militant when we said:

"Wages in Japan are much higher than yours. In fact, they're close to twice as much."

"You want me to believe that? Let's say what you say is true, but I hear you give up holidays to work. Free, private time is priceless to a man. Money can't buy it. Show us proof that freedom is not fettered in Japan."

"It is true, to be sure, that our use rate of paid holidays is about 40 percent and many give up their vacations, and workers work more overtime than you.[5] The last thing they think, though, is that they are being exploited by capitalists. Both the company and workers have faith in the prosperity, and our national economy itself has become powerful."

"Both company and nation are there so that we will have freedom and rest. But what is that if an individual is a pawn to them?"

"Oh, no, workers are better treated in certain ways in Japan. There is no distinction of lavatory or dining room between labor and management. No class distinctions—that's a certainty."

"Yes, there is. You have the emperor. I hear that you all work for the emperor. We work for the society in this country, and the society has classes, that's all."

"You have exceedingly large social discrimination. When business becomes slack in Japan, executives get a cut in their allowance first. And then it goes down to department or section chiefs in rank order. They either get a pay cut or a pay suspension. They won't give a pay cut to employees or let them wait at home until there is absolutely no way out of it. A lay-off is rarely practiced."

"Not giving a lay-off after asking them to give up a holiday? It's nothing to boast of. We don't stick to companies like parasites, to start with. If we lose hope in the company, we quit and find work somewhere else."

"They don't easily lose hope in the company in Japan. Employees are all capable of thinking and that helps produce high-quality products. We're different in that 96% of workers have graduated from high school and 38% from college. Their education helps improve what is old and defective and in this way they are making progress."

"There you go. You just confessed. This country hasn't changed a bit since the war. It's not necessary to change it. It has made progress as an industrially advanced nation. Japan has to make progress. This is how England is and this is how Japan has to be. There is a difference."

Our conversation was abruptly interrupted by Angela, a young woman representative:

"I hear many people live in company dorms or housing in Japan. They don't possess an independent mind. They sacrifice their freedom. To me, they are like race horses in the stable, kept for races. Not fired? Because they are horses, not people. It's no use arguing any further."

The meeting had turned into a madhouse once Angela began.

What Robertson and Angela claim and defend are representative of British values. It is welcomed that workers are not fired. But then, it is kindness—paternalism on the side of management and not a right on the side of labor. It is an all-out dependence to count on management kindness. One must be subordinate to management, giving up holidays, etc., to expect to be thus treated. This appears to be shabbiness and pathetic slavery in English eyes.

An essential credo for Robertson and Angela is not to depend on management. What they are to receive has to be specified as their right and validated by a contract. It is unthinkable for management to sacrifice itself and do something for employees. It will be too emotionally involved in a perplexing way, too. It is right and proper, therefore, for management to pursue a profit, and management can certainly lay off workers and eventually wreck a company if it is not gaining a profit. The company, as management sees it, does not exist for the benefit of employees. If so, it is a welfare institution, and that is not capitalism. Welfare should be covered by national taxes.

If the credo of Robertson and Angela is stretched even further, one will see a "hostile notion" of labor and management, not a sense of community. Management ought to pursue its profit and employees theirs. If a profit is gained out of hard work by workers, it should be returned to them. The logic that "company made a profit thanks to employees" cannot be approved. If we follow Robertson's logic, it is that workers gain less because management takes more. Workers gain more if management takes less. There are opposing interests between the two.

Both Robertson and Angela have no intention whatsoever of taking part in the objectives of the enterprise, only the intention of performing the work specified in the contract. They work for their own profit, not for the objectives of the enterprise. They take no interest in self-sacrifice other than what is in the contract, nor does management intend to offer more than it has promised.

There was one person at the discussion table who raised an objection to both Robertson and Angela. It was Thompson, shop steward. Thompson was struck with the feeling that labor-management relationships in Japan make an ideal Communist society. He was a Communist himself, but he does not think that Japanese management is acting out of favor only. A community of company performs its roles, and its gains are distributed as equally as possible. A community is a possibility only when each member performs his duty toward a realization of its objectives. It is not a community if it has opposing interests within itself.

A Japanese company actually is a community where some members are in charge of management and some are mechanics, each acting separately toward common profits. And the profits which belong to the community are distributed in accordance with each role. It is of significance that a pay cut starts with the executives in times of recession. It should not be looked upon as just kindness. Everybody needs a minimum amount of money to live. It is a very effective method of maintaining the lowest standard of living for all community members at the time of recession, certainly not the kindness. At least it is far superior to such a capitalistic society as England where the capitalist side takes the profits, however serious a recession is, and the remnants, if any, are distributed, but if there are none, no distribution is possible. Thompson concluded by saying: "Japan is not a capitalistic society, to say the least. It is a Communist society, and at that it seems to be the only Communist society on this whole earth."

DINING ROOM FOR EXECUTIVES

"Would you like to have some?" Maggie, a pretty and noble-looking girl, offered us a glass of sherry. The discussion session was over just at noon, and the survey team was invited to lunch in the third-floor executive dining room. Maggie, the only college graduate in T. Company, is a personnel manager. While we were enjoying the wine Maggie offered us, executives such as the accounting manager showed up one-by-one, and we all got into a conversation. Then President Bristle joined us. He took his seat at the table closest to the door. Various fruits—bananas, apples, oranges, and pears—were piled up on a nearby dish. Our lunch began with soup and biscuits, with various cheeses on the side. First the president took a biscuit and placed his favorite cheese on it. Each in turn filled his own plate with cheese and slid the plate to the next person. We found this amusing. The force of the plate made it stop abruptly in front of the next person, making an interesting game in itself.

I noticed, when we were about halfway through lunch, that all the dishes were very well timed, one after the other, and that a waitress never came to the tables. A bell was located under the table where the president was seated, and he apparently signaled the proper service.

We posed a question about dining rooms. They have three dining rooms, one of which is this dining room for executives, another for salaried workers, and another for hourly workers. Salaried and hourly workers have the same food, but hourly workers serve themselves at a long table. Salaried workers sit four at a table and have a waitress serving them. In every government office or company in Japan, we have tables like those for these hourly workers—two long tables put together to accommodate ten or so persons sitting facing each other. There is no dining by the classes.

T. Company also had three lavatories. The one for executives was a round room with a round mirror and carpeted floor, with a deodorizer provided. There is a strong tendency toward this state of affairs in England, and we find the same thing in America. Hourly workers usually use a different plant entrance from executives and even dress differently. It is generally easy to see the class differences in England: Executives wear ties, nonexecutives do not. This is a phenomenon never observed in Japan.

We were to call at the house of Mr. Thompson, from the first shift, at two in the afternoon on that day. He had made an offer to take us to his house himself from the company. He had been there waiting for us when we approached the executives' entrance. He had been seated directly on the bare front steps. It seemed to symbolize for us that he, a worker, was not allowed a step closer to the entrance for executives.

They have never gone on strike at T. Company, not once, which is a modern wonder. We were visiting Mr. Thompson's house to get his opinion on this topic. As a union leader on the shop floor, Mr. Thompson negotiates with management about complaints or improvements. His view on the advisability of a strike would carry weight. He responded to our inquiry of why workers have not gone on a strike with a smile:

There is no regulation that specifies that a strike is a must. Besides, not all companies or government and municipal offices in England have strikes. There are cases like us, exceptional, I admit, but we don't go on strike in spite of the fact that we may want to. Basically, we don't need one. We don't want a strike, because labor and management are getting along extremely well in T. Company. Our president, Mr. Bristle, is fully aware of our rights and he respects them. He has invested capital in safety facilities, to be specific, and our wages are comparable to neighboring companies or a little better. They are not bad, at the least. Yesterday, for example, a chap came to work drunk. I sent him home right away. I mean, I made up an excuse that he was not feeling well so that he wouldn't get a warning. A company that had little sympathy for us would surely have given him a warning.

It may be a minor point, but this is what we negotiated today: A man in the printing section is helping with a forklift after his work hours because of a shortage of hands. We are negotiating that this is not overtime and are trying to get management to acknowledge that he is a technician who can handle two categories of work. I am positive the company will acknowledge this. They are at least ready to acknowledge our rights as rights. Mr. Bristle plays fair with us in this sense. No, we don't need a strike. Doubtless, they are making a profit. One reason may be that our wages are lower compared to Japan. This doesn't mean we will give up a campaign for more wages.

I then asked, "What do you think about the system of class distinctions, such as in the dining room, lavatory, and entrance and exit?"

Surely, it is ridiculous. But it's just as ridiculous to go on a strike. They pursue their profits; we go after ours. Our profits simply boil down to asking for more wages. A company for us is but an instrument to gain wages. Our life is with the community or family. If their overdistribution to us makes it difficult to maintain their dining room, that's that. It's stupid to go on a strike just to wreck their dining room. It is a problem of the whole social system.

President Bristle, on the other hand, thinks of the participation of workers in the enterprise as near satisfactory. He feels it unrealistic to expect his workers to take part in the company as much as workers do in Japan.

During the oil crisis, the electricity was cut off three days a week in T. Company, and the machines were in operation only four days a week. It was a critical period for the company. Up until then, the machines had been in operation for twenty-four hours a day including Sundays. An interesting fact is that, in spite of a four-day operation, their productivity was as high as 90% of normal.

President Bristle learned that the crisis increased worker drive, but at the same time, he learned how little they worked ordinarily. Since then, he has devised several means to instigate the same amount of "drive" as during the oil crisis. He set a work norm and started a bonus system for those who exceeded it. Nonetheless, the result showed scarcely a change.

As Professor Robert Cole claims, high wages or other improvements in working conditions alone do not heighten workers' will to participate in company goals.[6] It is his dependence on the company that yields a strong will for participation. It is not only for wages or working conditions that a worker depends on the company, as we have already seen. The oil crisis made the Englishman get a taste of bankruptcy and realize his own self-destruction without his genuine dependence on the company. We can conclude then that his is a partial dependence only for wages.[7]

The willingness of T. Company was restored to the former state, once the oil crisis was over, the oil field in the North Sea turned out to be successful, which meant no more stoppage in power supply. This is all because T. Company functions merely as an instrument to gain wages in the mind of workers, as Mr. Thompson, shop steward, says.

INCIDENT OF THE ICE CREAM STAND

Professor Ronald Dore of England included the following interesting incident in his book, *The British Factory—Japanese Factory*:

There was an ice-cream seller who used to come and set up outside the gate, so we set up a stand inside—same Wall's ice-cream, same prices, only we had coloured umbrellas and seats. And people walked straight past it and bought their ice-cream outside.

Management went on and explained about the incident that took place at the Riverpool Plant of EE. Company: "We do have a dental surgery—after all, it *is* a time saver; we'd lose more time if people went outside, but hair—they can have their hair done any time."[8]

The first incident implied something that we should not overlook. The workers take the trouble to go out the gate to buy ice cream and are not interested in buying the kind the company has prepared. We can sense their hostile feeling against the company. In fact one youth declared: "You don't catch me putting a ha' penny into the pocket o' this firm." He meant that he would not spend even a half penny to the advantage of the company.

An analytical study of this fact by a personnel manager of a manufacturing company in England goes like this. British workers believe that a company's profit is equal to their loss. In short, the company is an enemy to them. The first thing that must have come to mind is that "the company is trying to make a profit by selling ice cream to us." Since the company is an enemy, they should not assist it. The last thing they think is that their own gains reflect the company's profits. Nor do they think that the company will do something for the workers' good. The reason why a dentist is kept, but not a barber, manifests this truth well. As a matter of fact, the priority order of distribution of profits in American and British management is first to the stockholders, second to executives, and last to the workers.

Due to the oil crisis, the Japanese industry had to be geared into slow economic growth in the 1970s from the higher growth of previous years. A so-called oversize bankruptcy turned up, and many enterprises began operating under reduced management. They tried to reduce waste and pare down personnel expenses. Some companies drove some personnel into voluntary retirement called shoulder-patting.[9] But few companies in Japan laid off as great a number of workers as in America or England to cope with the crisis.

Japanese companies responded to the crisis by first letting executives give up their remunerations. Next, came a pay cut for responsible persons like section chiefs. Workers in general scarcely experienced wage cuts. The same number of personnel on a smaller scale was the solution. Under this employment structure, there is no choice other than sharing the scanty amount. Corporations in which sharing the scanty amount did not help in dealing successfully with the recession were put on the brink of lay-offs or bankruptcy. American and British companies chose lay-offs without exception, filling the streets with the jobless. Japanese corporations appealed to the government, and yet another method was taken.

It is called employment insurance, which avoids dismissal of employees while the economy is poor. There was a flow of funds into the corporations from unemployment insurance which the government administers. It was a meager amount, but the corporations took pains so that workers were assured a minimum amount of wages on a lay-off. They showed a creditable recovery, without dismissing employees, along with a reduction in numbers by natural retirement and by willingness of the workers. Nearly two million workers shared in the benefit of the employment insurance.

Japanese workers look upon company profits as their own. The awareness was made all the more intense during the recession caused by the oil crisis. Natural trust between a corporation and its employees is what underlies the willingness system. Companies depend on employees and employees on companies.

Zenith Radio Corporation, an American TV manufacturer, once laid off 5,600 workers across the Zenith plants in the country. *Forbes* magazine ran a follow-up survey of 1,500 workers at four Zenith plants in the Chicago area.[10] Contacts were made with random samples of former Zenith workers. Seventy percent of the workers contacted had gone back to work in thirty-one months. About 3.5% were out of the labor force. The remaining 26.3% were still unemployed and receiving unemployment compensation. What has become of their lives since then?

One of them, Ramon Valle, forty-three years old, was laid off after working for twenty-three years. His weekly wages of $263 dropped to $175—solely from unemployment compensation. He is the breadwinner of his family of a wife and four children, and he passes the time with his camera, tropical fish, and tape cassettes. He talks about lay-off as follows: "To be 'laid-off' is to be given false hope."

PART II

Mechanisms of Willingness to Work

5

Willingness and Anxiety

IF IT IS COUNTED AS LATE, MAKE IT A PAID HOLIDAY

In an earlier account, Mr. Robertson had headed straight for the rest quarters and started enjoying his tea and pipe on top of being late. He was only two minutes late. The reason for his action was that fifteen minutes' worth of pay would be deducted from his wages because his pay is calculated in fifteen-minute units. Mr. Robertson would have worked thirteen minutes for nothing.

I brought up this case when I had a conversation with a personnel manager of H. Company in Japan. The manager then told me that quite a few of his employees ask him to "make the day a paid holiday" when they come to work late. And that they still work nearly all day and some even work overtime. They are not normally paid for the overtime.

When they say, "make it a paid holiday," they are exercising their right to an entitled holiday.[1] There is no way for them to get paid for overtime, because they are officially on vacation. There is no monthly overtime pay with a monthly salary. There was one case of a government office paying some overtime on holidays. They got a bad reputation for allotting overtime pay, regardless of the actual overtime work. What is the psychological mechanism to "work," though on a paid holiday? Here seems to lie a key to the "willingness to work."

H. Company does not use a time clock. The employees are expected to report their own tardiness. This is one difference from American and British companies, but there is another essential one. There is no deduction of pay for tardiness in most companies in Japan. The situation is quite unlike the one in which Mr. Robertson is placed. Instead, "late once" is written in a worker's personal record. An entry of one tardiness in the personal record has no official effect on a worker. If it did, it might affect their bonus calculation in a minor way. Since there is no stipulation that specifies a reduction of bonus in case of lateness, however, we must say that the entry carries no official sanction.

The influence then is something less than official. Being late once is an indication that one is a lazy worker. Again there is no disciplinary provision that specifies a pay cut or demotion in cases of tardiness. It may result in a personal evaluation by personnel managers or simply affect one's reputation among fellow workers. It amounts to being on the blacklist. There is no substantive result from a reputation of being lazy. It concerns personnel matters to be on the blacklist, and one will be placed under strong pressure. If it has a direct relation to a concrete penalty, it creates a certain fear in him, but when it is over, it is over. Besides, the penalty is clearly shown, and one should know how to cope with it. But being on the blacklist, the worker cannot but lose his peace of mind because he is not sure how it will affect him. This fear is more or less transitory, and he can be prepared to cope with it. It is obvious, but there is no help for anxiety. There is only a vague idea of what troubles to expect. Anxiety can be actualized quickly, too. Besides being ambiguous, it may be endless. Furthermore, the real substance of anxiety is "an anxious feeling that is brought about when a value accepted as essential is threatened."[2] A worker will stop being uneasy only when he quits work, but he is under no obligation to do that, because it is "essential" for this individual to do so. Here lies a difference among Japanese, American, and British workers. One tardiness gives rise to vague misgivings, which threatens something essential in the habitual latecomers.

What does it imply, then? That the Japanese worker exercises his right for a paid holiday instead of going to the rest quarters? As we have already seen, the rate of using a paid holiday in Japan is only 40%. There will be plenty left even if he makes use of one more paid holiday. This is easily comprehended; he gets the same evaluation whether he takes four or five out of twenty paid holidays. But ten minutes of lateness will label him as a lazy worker. We cannot pinpoint why. Our guess is that it is because he did not plan it or he caused only a small degree of trouble to the work. An abrupt absence and an abrupt lateness are both unwelcome. The shop floor is no place for a lazy "bum." In essence, coming late resembles chattering, loafing, or taking frequent breaks. It is desecration of the workplace, in a word. The person is not yet mentally prepared to work; if not, he is better off absent.

A lazy bum now has turned into an eager beaver, actually working, sometimes working overtime, while exercising the right of a paid holiday. He has made a splendidly effective use of his lateness. In this sense, it pays, by all means, to work on a paid holiday.

True, Mr. Robertson acted quite differently from workers of H. Company in Japan, but there is an element common to both: They acted for the benefit of individuals if their employment structure is taken into consideration. It seems that their different actions can be attributed to different employment structures. What you find ultimately behind the employment structures are thinness or weakness of linkage between organization and workers in the hourly worker system, on the one hand, and firmness or solidity between the two in the monthly worker system, on the other. What implications do they have, after all?

Employment structure seems to be intimately related to willingness. Are the Japanese not too dependent on the organization? Consequently, a onetime lateness weighs heavily on a worker's mind. If we can elucidate the principle at work, an incentive to the Japanese willingness will be made clear. We have already commented on Professor Cole's analysis. He has described it as a total dependence of employees on the organization.

Much can be settled and explained by assuming that willingness is associated with employment structure, but that doesn't appear to be all there is to it. A Japanese salaried worker is, no doubt, loyal to his company because he knows being fired would ruin his career. So, he has patience, guts, and tolerance, which is commonly said to be the essence of willingness. There is something else, though, which loyalty and tolerance cannot explain. Take the example of the spring device in a previous chapter; it is not explained by loyalty and tolerance alone. What then? In the latter half of the book we will throw light upon the willingness in relation to Japanese employment structure and the willingness that stems from the Japanese personality and culture.

MIRACLE AT TARRYTOWN

Tarrytown Plant is an assembly-line plant of GM, which has quite unexpectedly been brought into focus in recent years. In connection with automotive productivity in America, Tarrytown Plant is becoming a symbol for such catchwords as "We are as good as the Japanese," or "We can do it, too." There has been a strong social impetus to learn from Japanese productivity or superior quality of products, since an issue has been made of the inferior quality of American cars. Such comparisons were made in a TV program, "If Japan Can . . . , Why Can't We?" produced by NBC, one of the three major TV networks.

Other examples are an article "American Workers Are As Good" by Professor Cole, University of Michigan, and an article "Americans Are Not As Good," a counter argument by Professor Odawara of Sophia University, for both of which the *Nippon Keizai Shimbun* has spared pages. Professor Cole is a scholar of business organizations as well as a prominent scholar on Japan and has conducted valuable surveys both in Japan and America.

Professor Cole cited Tarrytown Plant as one way of proving that American labor quality is as good as that of Japan. Here is what he says:

Let us take the illustrative case of General Motors, Tarrytown Plant. Located in the suburbs of New York City, a great many black and Puerto Rican workers with little education had been employed in the early '70s. This plant had been ranked lowest among GM assembly line plants in terms of productivity and quality of products. GM was seriously considering closing it down, but started the group training program for all workers, inclusive of problem solving method, in 1976. It was based on the results of experiments performed during 1972 and 1973. The problem solving method is what was evolved out of QC (Quality Control) circles in Japanese factories.

The result was remarkable. The plant jumped from GM's worst assembly line plant to one of its best, judging from the criteria of productivity and quality of products and so on. The workers became enthusiastic about making devices in many ways. Labor-management relationships improved conspicuously and worker grievances showed a sudden drop.[3]

What Professor Cole maintains is that it has become one of the best plants, learning from QC circles in Japan, and that this achievement was made with the cooperation of the poorly educated blacks and Puerto Ricans. Therefore, he concludes that the American workers are as good as the Japanese. We must accept what took place as fact. The question is, though, we do not know whether the result came about solely from the group training program. Neither do we know why the program was accepted. Fortunately, *Time* magazine (May 5, 1980) has some comments on Tarrytown Plant, which we can examine more closely.

Detroit continues to struggle with the dark reputation that it turns out cars inferior to those made by Japanese or West German manufacturers and that American workers are not sufficiently productive. But one Big Three plant belies such notoriety. The General Motors factory in Tarrytown, N.Y., one of the plants where the company assembles its hot-selling front-wheel-drive Chevrolet Citation, has earned the reputation of being perhaps the giant automaker's most efficient assembly facility. Tarrytown's current renown is more surprising because in the early 1970's the 55–year-old plant was infamous for having one of the worst labor-relations and poorest quality records at GM.

The turnaround at Tarrytown grew out of the realization by local management and union representatives that inefficiencies and industrial strife threatened the plant's continued operation. Automakers sometimes use forced plant closing caused by sluggish auto sales to unload a lemon facility. Ford, for example, decided two weeks ago to shut the gates of its huge Mahwah, N.J., plant largely because it had a poor quality record. After Tarrytown lost a truck production facility in 1971, *bosses and workers became fearful for their jobs and got together to find better ways to build cars*. (Emphasis added)[4]

It has to be noted, however, that Tarrytown Plant did not show a speedy recovery. It suffered 7% absenteeism as before, and an unprecedented number of disciplinary and dismissal notices were given. Looking back upon those days, the former United Auto Workers shop chairman at Tarrytown commented that it sure was a "hell of a battleground."

Tarrytown made a comeback, nonetheless. The biggest contributing factor was the cooperation between labor and management as the adoption of QC circles exemplifies. Of all the factors that promoted the labor-management cooperation, the imminence of the factory closing was the greatest. They were in imminent danger of losing jobs because of the oil crisis, which was observed in Japan, too. Workers had been deprived of freedom to change their jobs due to the downturn of the American automotive industry. GM workers in Tarrytown were about to be struck by full unemployment.

Workers at Tarrytown Plant got up their drive because there were no other alternatives to dependence on the plant. There was no complete assurance that the threat of a closedown or lay-off would operate as a driving force toward willingness. In Ford's Mahwah Plant, which appears in the article in *Time*, the truck line was closed in 1979, and then the whole plant the next year. The twenty-five-year history of Mahwah Plant came to an end with as many as 5,000 workers out of jobs.

I want to call attention to the fact that the Tarrytown spirit was not observed in Mahwah. They had come face to face with the crisis of a closedown of the passenger car line (the truck line was already closed). It was also reported that the plant reeked of the smell of marijuana and was never free from theft.[5]

Probably because American workers do not place too much value in depending on the company, the crisis of unemployment does not always act as an incentive for them to work willingly. They are probably under the social structure and social awareness that unemployment does not lead to loss of the means to make a living. For the Japanese, the organization they belong to is the base and center of life. The Japanese workers depend on it for income, human relations, and social life. If a Japanese worker leaves his company, not only will he be in financial straits, but he will also be excluded from good friends, sports, and hobby activities. In terms of social life, it means that he is not allowed to carry calling cards or business cards. Then, people generally give him cold shoulders, whatever good ideas he may present. Put simply, he is even deprived of membership in society.

Ex-workers of Ataka Sangyo, a trading company, bear witness to this phenomenon when their company went into large-scale bankruptcy and was absorbed by C. Itoh Company. It is reported that fewer than half were transferred to C. Itoh Company, but many of them said it was hellish either to leave or to stay on.

The effects of unemployment caused by bankruptcy go into many areas and fall within essential matters. The case of Tarrytown certainly proves, as Professor Cole points out, that there is something common between the United States and Japan, but the case like Mahwah is what we generally observe on the American scene. We should regard Tarrytown as an exception. Unemployment in Japan concerns something basic, much more so than in the case of automotive workers in America. Employment structure is the nucleus and an essential part of the social structure. The Japanese workers, more than Tarrytown Plant workers, are basically dependent on the company. We should say, in the case of Japanese workers, that this willingness stems largely from this dependence.

Shichihei Yamamoto has an excellent insight on this relationship between company and individuals—worker dependence on the company in Japan. He points out that the company is a functional group that pursues profits rationally, on the one hand, but, on the other, it is a community of organizational members.[6] If we take the view that an individual is dependent on the company, we are not describing organization and individual as anything more than opponents to each other, strictly by the yardstick of Americans or Europeans. By the Japanese yardstick, a company organization is a community of members. Banishment from a community differs essentially from losing means of financial source. Yamamoto goes on:

Many mashers are not guilty of criminal offense even if they are handed over to the police. Being a personal behavior off the job, it has nothing to do with the company as a functional group, and the company has undergone no damage. Even if a masher's behavior is publicized in the newspaper, it will give rise to no trouble if the offender is a bum, for instance, and has nothing to do with the honor of the community. But if he is a "company species" belonging to an established community, in the first place, he has no basis for a plea against banishment because he has "affected the honor of the company." What is implied is that, if the offender sues the company for unfair dismissal, his honor is even more thoroughly blotted out by the related society.[7]

What Yamamoto describes above is the substance and function of the community. We have to note here that he is in the wrong in that he thinks the masher is "not found guilty." The act of masher falls under public indecency and is a criminal offense. It is off the point here, though, and his argument is precisely right in that banishment from a community has a more effective function as a disciplinary measure than criminal punishment. It can be considered a matter of great importance that bringing disgrace upon one's company leads to being blotted out of the related society.

Among developed industrial countries, Japan has an extremely low incidence of crime. Crime patterns are different from country to country, which makes an exact comparison difficult, but a rough comparison between America and Japan shows that the number of thefts and burglaries in the United States is several times higher than that of Japan. This puzzles criminologists a great deal. Doubtless, a community of company, which Yamamoto describes, works as a deterrent.

An organization in Japan is a community and the nucleus of life for an individual. It is even an ethical group that has influence in deterring crime. A life apart from it is unthinkable not only financially but also socially and mentally.

As stated before, tardiness has more than just financial meaning in Japan. Man has desires for belonging, respect from others, besides a desire for economic stability. Nevertheless, being two minutes late has no more meaning than a fifteen-minute wage cut for Mr. Robertson. Even if Mr. Robertson gets dismissed after getting warnings for tardiness, he will be accepted in other groups, for the other company is an economic functional group, not a community. As the article in the *Wall Street Journal* pointed out, Mahwah Plant in the United States partly consists of drug addicts and thieves and is not an ethical group by any means, nor is it a community. Turnover is always a possibility, thus Robertson is never dismissed from *all* social groups.

The case is different in a Japanese company. Lateness labels a worker as a lazy bum in a community. An employee of H. Company is placed under some pressure which obliges him to work after proposing to "make it a paid holiday." He does not get a wage cut for sure, but he will be left uneasy. The question is carried over to the future. The chances are that he plays second fiddle to his fellow workers or is relegated to a trivial post or, in turn, has to leave the organization. In brief, essential problems for an individual remain behind.

Relegation is a fundamental matter and concerns his whole life because the organization is the base and center of his life. What is in the background is very little chance of drifting away from the organization. Job change is taboo for the Japanese. He cannot live outside the organization; he is totally dependent on it. Those who suffer from lack of promotion may even commit suicide.

Seen from the aspect that the community controls the individual, we can say that Japanese willingness is stipulated by total dependence on the organization to which one belongs, such as H. Company, Ministry of X., or Y. City Hall. Being dependent is only leaning against others. Dependence is opposite from independence. Being dependent, one does not regard the organization as a means of living. Being independent, one regards the organization as a means of gaining wages, a means that can be replaced. If one does not like it, one can find other means, i.e., another organization.

An ingenious use of anxiety will work as an incentive to work. But an incentive for Americans and the British (of whom Robertson is typical) has to be convincing enough as a means. A good offer like high wages and short work hours is very potent. Since means can be substituted, organizations rival each other in offering good conditions. But a Japanese organization is not just a means of making a living; it is an object in itself. Moreover, the object is life itself. There can be no substitution for it, for that would be self-destruction.

It is true that the social structure stipulates Japanese willingness for the most part, but not all of it. We will ultimately touch upon the values that support the employment structure. Even though a high rate of turnover is seen among blue-collar workers, Japanese corporations maintain high levels of productivity. The pressure due to not-easy-to-do job change alone cannot account for it. What is it, then?

DON'T TAKE A JOB AWAY FROM THE JANITOR

The instant the assembly line came to a halt, everybody went home with their tools or appliances all scattered around. It is no wonder, as this is at Y. Company in England which produced Chaplin and his movie *Modern Times*. Nobody put the tools back into the tool box, nor did anybody clean up. This must be troublesome to the next shift. There is even the possibility of injury if metal scraps are not cleaned up.

In Japan, on the other hand, everybody gives a polish to his tools, puts them back where they belong, mops the floor, then goes home when the line stops. In some plants this operation is practiced during work hours and, in some others, after work hours (thus it is done for no pay). In more and more cases, janitorial services are now hired to clean in Japan, following the Western example. Nevertheless, the number of cases are few among private companies. Some government offices are economizing and do their own cleaning, but in most cases, they leave the job to janitorial services. In every country, it is a practice to clean and polish personal machines, although janitorial services take care of the rest, such as commonly used areas, corridors, toilets, etc.

I made an inquiry of Harv at Yakima Plant of W. Company in the U.S. as to why they do not clean up. He immediately answered: "That will offend the janitors. They'll call us thieves." We made the same inquiry of many employees at Y. and T. companies in England and got similar answers: "It's not my job," or "That will put somebody else out of work," or "That means I'm stealing their wages." Some even said that cleaning their machines is not part of their job in the strict sense of the word, that it is the job of the maintenance section, since it has to do with keeping the machines in good condition. In contrast, in Yokohama Plant of H. Company in Japan, all workers mop the floor and clean windows after a day's work is done. Even difficult-to-reach windows are handled by the male employees themselves.

Then we put the same question which we had asked Harv to the Japanese workers: "Is it part of your duty to clean the shop?"

Most of them said, "Well, it's hard to say," instead of giving a definite answer. One said, "We're naturally responsible for it. It's only a matter of cleaning, isn't it?" We further asked him where to find the document that specifies his responsibility for the cleaning or whether there was any such regulation. He guessed, finally, that we might find something in the rules of general affairs about it.

Yokohama Plant of H. Company has a certain definition as to the work and scope of responsibility and uses it as a guiding principle. It goes as follows: " 'Job' is something you find on your own."

Labor relations manager, Mr. H., gave us a many-sided explanation about the way plant workers work. Most worthwhile improvements in his plant are predominantly done by the specialists like design engineers, who are more or less in charge. It is their job as specialists. It sometimes happens, interestingly enough, that a worker on the shop floor comes up with a suggestion for some improvements and imparts it to a specified person in the design section. This gives an engineer ideas, which may lead to a drastically cost-cutting change. Several such experiences have been reported in the past.

In such cases, men on the shop floor are not given credit for the matter. What is more important is that the specified engineer, who was inspired by the suggestion, wrestles with the work as his own. Sometimes the work involves other sections. "Job is indeed something you find on your own."

A general scope of "job" is to be found on one's own, but it is a general scope and nothing more. The company target of improving quality and increasing productivity while lowering costs has been internalized by many employees. An exception is again observed in younger workers. Suppose the plant is working for a target: deliver 5,000 machines to a country in Southeast Asia within the month of August. In order to achieve the goal, the calculated production goals and deadlines are given to each team. Being partitioned according to the team, the goal is put up on the walls or notice boards all over the factory. In order to carry through the goal, many are obliged to work overtime. This brings about a problem. Young workers would not work overtime unless they are specifically ordered to. It is an overtime order, but sometimes the superior may ask them in a low-key way, "Will you please work over-time today, Mr. A?" Most of the time, they get sulky and say, "Again?" No, they will not work overtime willingly. Though some younger work-ers are reluctant, workers as a whole try to grapple with the goal voluntarily.

The above scene will probably be what you will find in the Japanese plants on the average. The scenes form a remarkable contrast with those in the United States and England. The workers in these countries do not clean the shops as described before. Their work role is clear-cut, and they play it out faithfully. No one will come up with an im-provement plan beyond the scope of his responsible area, unless asked. They do not work overtime unless ordered to. The required amount of work for the company does not agree with their required amount of work. Their standard of judgment for work is whether it yields the necessary pay. They decide whether to work overtime or not according to their economic needs. The work necessary for the company may not agree with their needs as persons.

The required amount of work for the company does agree with the required amount of work of the Japanese workers when we compare how the work is carried out. The nature of work necessary for the company agrees with the work of an individual beyond his presupposed work role. In the case of American and British workers, the amount of work necessary for the company, whatever it is or whatever amount it is, is not equal to the work of an individual. In Japan, both the company and individual measure the amount of necessity against the yardstick common between the two; whereas they do not have a com-mon yardstick in the United States and England. The difference can be explained in part by how the company is dependent on individuals. Expenses of hiring cleaners will accumulate as a loss for both company and individuals, and eventually workers' share of profits will decrease. But financial reasons alone do not logically explain the Japanese work-ers' cleaning and sustained patience seen in their daily overtime work. If it is an overtime allowance that they strive toward, they will even-tually want more leisure instead of more income as in the case of American and British workers. Some Japanese youths hold the same values as their Western counterparts, but in most cases they volunteer to work overtime even when they are not particularly in need of money. What is the mentality behind this?[8]

WHAT A VOLUNTEER REALLY IS

Once I wanted to include in a survey a question as to whether or not people work overtime or participate in suggestion programs as

volunteers in Japan, the United States, and England. A voluntary act
is a gratuitous act accompanied by some sacrifice. People engage en-
ergetically in volunteer activities in America and England. Housewives talk about such-and-such "voluntary activity" rather proudly.
People place a high value on volunteerism as an act of social consciousness. Also, one has to be "well-to-do" to be a volunteer. Being a
volunteer sometimes works as a means of having economic superiority
recognized.

An American woman, for example, asked that the fact she works
part time be kept secret and then spoke with pride to others about her
volunteer activity elsewhere. No other example accounted for volunteerism better than this.

Quite a few people work overtime as volunteers in Japan. It is vol-
unteering of a sort to give up a paid holiday and work. Extraordinarily,
some companies once purchased paid holidays. It is true that a sacrifice
for the company is made when the right to paid holidays is not exercised. We thought it necessary for our comparative study in Japan, the
United States, and England to find out facts about possible voluntary
overtime.

Our original plan met with opposition in America. The claim was
that there existed no such notion as working as a volunteer in the
business firms. Voluntary activity is an act of goodwill without compensation, to begin with, toward those in need of assistance. From
American values in general, a company cannot be an object of voluntary
activity. More explicitly, they say that why on earth should one have
to render free services to a company which exploits them. How in the
world can one give services free to an exploiting party? It just was not
logically possible.

This defiant attitude made us take a closer look at the giving-up of
paid holidays and overtime work for no pay in Japan. Employees and
their organizations are not the least opposed to each other; both are
formed into a single whole, sharing the same objectives. This makes
it possible, from the level of rights and duties, for each party to make
self-sacrificing actions.

As a result of a preliminary survey in America, we found it impossible to use the term *volunteer* to describe this cooperative attitude.
An alternative proposal was the use of "willingly." Goodwill forms the
basis, because when people work willingly, they work of their own
accord—voluntarily as opposed to reluctantly. We see some similarity
there with a voluntary act, since it is not an ordered act. The only
difference between being a volunteer and being willing is that the latter
gets paid, the former does not. The pay factor could be a decisive influence, and we were anxious to discover the outcome. Figure 6 shows

**Figure 6.   Japanese Work Overtime Willingly; Americans Work
Overtime for the Pay**

"Did you work overtime willingly (with no mention of pay)?"

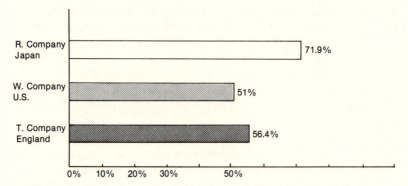

"Did you work willingly because there was a lot of work to be done
apart from the pay?"

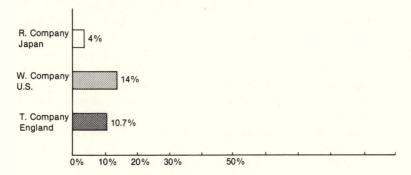

the result: 72% in R. Company in Japan, 51% in W. Company in the
United States, and 56% in T. Company in England worked overtime
"willingly."

The percentage is highest in Japan, but it is also high in the United
States and England. The question asked was merely whether workers
worked willingly, with no mention of pay. What the percentages probably show is that workers *worked willingly in order to make money.*
Therefore, our next step was to ask them whether they worked willingly because there was a lot of work to be done apart from the pay.
The result is also shown in figure 6.

Four percent of R. Company in Japan, 14% of W. Company in the
United States, and 11% of T. Company in England answered that the

amount of work was not an important factor. (To put it another way, money is the primary object.) In summary, we can assume that Japanese workers worked overtime of their own accord because there was so much work to be done, not because of money. This difference between Japan, the United States, and England suggests something fundamental. People in Japan work overtime because "work requires them to do so" as we have seen before. *Work* is the deciding factor for judgment. In America and England, on the other hand, this factor plays an extremely weak role. The yardstick that "work requires them" implies that the company is not a place or means for monetary gains.

A similar situation to this can be found in home-life where it occurs that some necessary measure has to be taken: A fuse has to be replaced after it is blown out; roses have to be watered; or one has to take books home for the children. These situations essentially resemble the one in which a Japanese worker will find himself. On the one hand, there is an act of sacrifice by one party for the other; it means that one's decisions are in response to the situation.

It concerns an essential part of human behavior to act sacrificially for the company, leaving personal profit out of it; and that decision depends on the situation, not on personal will.

What desires underlie this mentality? There might be a desire for social recognition as a member of a company-oriented society for the person compelled to finish work he sees loaded in front of him. There might be a desire for self-actualization through work, which could be called the traditional climate in Japan. Of course, several days of overtime in succession, especially when it involves repetitious labor, can be painful. In order to endure the pain, a mere desire for self-training would hardly provide enough motivation to overcome an easy-going spirit. One needs a self-denying spirit or a strong "will" to put up with the hardship.

A motivational analysis of values will have to be done to clarify what constitutes worthwhile actions and what does not. Desire to finish work, desire for a sense of accomplishment, etc., are all possibilities for explanation of what composes willingness.

6

Acceptance and Rejection

THE SECRET OF MR. BREAKMOOR'S BIG PROMOTION

Mr. Breakmoor, a cracker-jack salesman, who used to work at a St. Louis factory, was promoted to the marketing department of the main office. He had an outstanding business record. Says Mr. Breakmoor, "This is just an example":

In his St. Louis days, he had a customer who used to wrap his products with cardboard but made a claim one day that the cardboard tore, spilling the contents. He saw the actual package and understood the cause. Cardboard is easy to tear crosswise, but resists tear lengthwise. Mr. Breakmoor immediately took corrective measures, by asking the man in charge of the plant to cut the cardboard longer crosswise, instead of lengthwise. Likewise he instructed the customer to staple the package vertically indicating also that no other change would be necessary for the wrapping. No more torn cardboard incidents occurred thereafter, much to the customer's satisfaction, and Mr. Breakmoor had deservedly won the loyalty of the customer.

Using this case as an example, he told us these secrets of his sales business: First and foremost, you must have good communication with your customer, and have good knowledge of how your product is being used. Some young salespersons, he says, never take the trouble even to telephone their customers and, instead, idle away their time. Most basic of all are phone calls. It is part of your job to make phone calls, and you should never spare yourself that trouble. It is not necessarily part of your job or responsibility to find out how your product is put to use after delivery, but this is another important factor. It seemed to be the secret of secrets. He was successful because he actually looked into it and listened intently to what the customers had to say. After hearing him talk, I felt assured that Mr. Breakmoor was climbing the ladder of success.

Now another scene. It was at a company near Liverpool in England.

An air-conditioner was ordered about a month ago, and the machine had not been completely installed yet. After the order was placed, an electrician examined the installation site, source of electric power, and wiring. In about a week, the air-conditioner was delivered to the plant. It took nearly two weeks for the machine to be installed in position. The electrical work and inspection are still unfinished. Almost a month has passed since the day of order, but the air-conditioner is not operating.

This is a typical situation whenever orders are placed for anything in England. Subdivision of labor is one explanation for it: Salesmen sell, carpenters do carpentry, electricians do electrical work, inspectors inspect, and so forth. This is unlike electrical appliance stores in Akihabara, where just about everything is expertly handled.[1] These stores are, so to speak, jacks-of-all-trades.

Subdivision of work is found in government offices in Japan to some degree. "We do not handle it in our office" is what we often hear. Government offices are vertically subdivided. One municipal office once created a "Right-Away Department" and enjoyed great popularity. They showed, as it were, "the willingness after the fashion of Mr. Breakmoor."

Being an everyday affair in England, the case of the air-conditioner is not noteworthy. It has been described as English malaise. The malaise is caused by the line being distinctly drawn between work. The Englishmen call it the "demarcation line." The dictionary defines it as "a line or marking of a boundary," and it is literally the line never to be infringed upon like the Maginot Line between Germany and France in World War II and the 38th parallel between North Korea and the Republic of Korea.

In America, the line is fixed and drawn in the job description. Shortly after the war, the idea of job description was introduced in Japan, and a general range of duties was specified but never carried out as written. In America, though, we can asume that the range is faithfully followed. An American personnel manager once whispered into my ear his personal opinion of it:

Job description in America is not as rigorous as you people think. In my personal opinion, it is more or less an outside display for recruitment. No girl will accept the job if "serving coffee" is included in the job description. The trick is not to mention coffee serving at the time of recruiting of female workers.

It amused me a lot when he prepared coffee himself, saying, "My secretary is out for the moment." He came in holding a paper cup in each hand with a cigar in his mouth. His hands being full, the ashes from his cigar dropped in the coffee, making a hissing sound. He said with a wink, "A job description should never include coffee serving." His subordinates answered explicitly that serving coffee is not included in their duties. It is either to be regretted, or should we say that his strategy has been a success. In response to our question, "Have you done anything that is outside the scope of your job? If yes, what is it?" one respondent put down "served coffee."

In addition to serving coffee, we found many other jobs outside the scope of their duties, as indicated in the responses. This suggested that job description was not strictly followed. As we shall see later, though, the situation in America differs greatly from that of Japan. In their case, we can say, work performed is more restricted than in Japan.

What Mr. Breakmoor told us as a secret is that he went beyond his duties to see the actual situation of the users, struck on a profitable idea, and offered it to them. As far as his primary scope of duties goes, he could have gotten by just selling the products. He did not have to present his idea to the user. But he went out of his way to help them and succeeded. Mr. Breakmoor's secret is not a secret at all, however, for a Japanese salesman of corrugated cardboard. He would rather call it "kid stuff," not a secret. In every plant of R. Company in Japan, we come across several certificates of gratitude from the customers. These are the rewards salespersons receive in return for the splendid ideas they have presented to their customers. I was surprised to find how these salespersons actually went about their business. They even participated in QC circles of their customers and contributed whatever information they had to them as though they were employed there. No wonder customers send in certificates of gratitude or commendation.

One explanation for high productivity and innovation in Japan, as this example shows, is the stretching out of the scope of work instead of limiting it. The guiding principle of H. Company in Japan, "Job is something one finds on his own," contributes to this outlook of stretching out the scope of work. The above-mentioned demarcation line, which is considered to be one of the causes of English malaise, does nothing more than limit the scope of work.

We might be able to say that limiting the scope of work is unproductive and stretching it out is productive. Stretching out the scope of work accounts very well for high economic growth in Japan and vitality that overcame the oil crisis. At some point after the war, American management technique was introduced in Japan, and most of the corporations adopted job descriptions. In so doing, they established clearcut lines of authority and responsibility. Because remnants of the practice still exercise influence, Japanese workers tend to look at the scope of job even more rigorously than workers do in the United States. However, as shall be discussed below, this is confined to the "scope of written rules," and the actual "scope of work" goes far beyond.

The actual scope of work in Japan is comprehensive and diffuse as in the case of salespersons of corrugated cardboard. Salesmen should boast of their salesmanship, their sales records. They should be free to make phone calls or participate in the QC circles of their customers.

What will account for the stretching and restricting views of the scope of work? In spite of the introduction of the American job description system, the existing practice in Japan actually goes beyond the system. This makes us assume the existence of more powerful regulations than those of job description, which are supported by traditional culture. We might say that it is something closely connected to willingness.

MAGNA CARTA FOR BLUE-COLLAR WORKERS

"I helped those who were behind schedule, because I love T. Company." No, this was not in Japan. It was written by an employee of T. Company in England. If the company objectives have been internalized among workers, they will work even at the cost of their own profits. Prime Minister Margaret Thatcher or managers would be very pleased to hear this and would say that it is the very spirit that would rescue England. From the viewpoint of limited scope of work, you are not allowed to help others. But the above-quoted employee helped the others out of his love for the company. Details are not specified, so there is no way to know how much burden he shouldered. From the Japanese value standard, it seems to be nothing special to be excited about. Let us make a further examination.

"Helping those who are behind schedule" is an act naturally expected and actually practiced in Japan, it seems. We asked several questions concerning the scope of work:

1. Is the scope of work clearly specified?
2. Do you keep strictly to the scope of work?
3. If you go beyond the scope of work, what is it?

If the company objectives have been internalized, the scope of work is considered not to be limited. Much work beyond the scope will actually be done.

Originally, job description was a result of managerial demand to make the work compact. It is a management concern if there is work under nobody's charge. Taylor's theory of management is composed of the grasping of the work, the integration of it, and the allotting of limited work to each worker. As a result, the responsibility of each worker is made clear, and the work is performed smoothly as a whole. However, the underlying principle of the theory is the fragmentation and specification of work. This line of thinking went very well with the idea of individualism, which makes clear individual rights and responsibility.

Specifying the scope of work fulfills one more function as well as clarifying individual responsibility. It is exemption from responsibility which is out of one's scope of work. The relation here will be equal to the one between the law and citizens. The criminal code, for instance, is often said to be a Magna Carta for criminals; that is, any action not stipulated in the criminal code will not inflict a penalty on them. In this sense, citizens' rights are protected against only those actions previously stipulated by the criminal code.

Similarly, job description is a Magna Carta for factory workers. No punishment will be inflicted upon them for not doing work other than what is stipulated. Keeping to the description, a worker will never be called a lazy bum, will get his promotion, and will receive no pay cut. The idea in modern labor management (by Taylor and others) is never to expect more jobs to be done than what are described. Managerial power comes into play if more work other than what is stipulated in the description is to be expected. It ought to be enough for work to be allotted first by scientific analysis.

The Taylor method is never perfect, as success in Japan shows. Rather, we think specifying the scope of work is tentative. It is of consequence to perform the necessary work in cooperation with each other, taking away the demarcation line, if the company objectives have been internalized. Let us further our discussion on these premises.

Is the scope of work clearly specified? The results from the first question were quite surprising. Japan had the highest number of answers, "Yes, the work is specified." As figure 7 shows, 70% in R. Company in Japan, only 10% in W. Company in the United States, and 60% in T. Company in England answered in the affirmative.

The U.S. figure surprised us, too. As many as 51% answered "not specified," and as many as 33.3% answered "I don't know." The figure was large in T. Company in England, too. As many as 26.3% answered "not specified." What in the world does this mean?

We went over the questionnaires to see if there was any mistake in translation. None was found. The fact seemed true. Personnel manager of W. Company commented that in his opinion job description was for recruitment purposes. The facts here seem to support his opinion. It is possible that some jobs not specified in the job description are performed—either ordered or out of custom. This might put employees under the impression that work is not specified. Having never given rise to quarrel with union leaders, as far as we know, it must fall under trivial matters. Then we made an inquiry of the corrugate machine operator mentioned before to confirm the fact. After saying, "They certainly gave me one, in fact I have it here. I will go and get it," he

Figure 7.   Job Descriptions Are More Specific in Japan

"Is the scope of work clearly specified?" (Percentages reflect "yes" answers.)

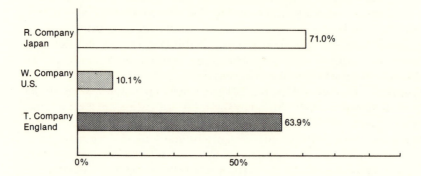

brought typewritten sheets to us. His job was specified on two pages. He gave an explanation that all his work was not enumerated there, that it was approximate. He also added that it never works out as it is specified and that he has to work at various other jobs in order to make good headway with his own work. To be sure, the specification is written without attention to details such as being in the factory fifteen minutes before work starts and certain points to be attended to. We can say that it is for recruiting. It is inclusive of all general procedures, though it says operation of the corrugate machine.

No corresponding job description is found in Japan, interestingly enough. They are probably only conscious of operating a corrugate machine. A previous arrangement might be necessary before the next shift takes their turn. Whether to come to work fifteen minutes earlier is up to them to judge.

It is becoming clear that a difference of interpretation is seen between Japanese workers and American and British workers in deciding whether "the work is clearly specified." A Japanese worker on the shop floor will consider that his scope of work is within the Suzuki team, the first shift, and that he is to operate the corrugate machine. He is made conscious that "the work is clearly specified" if he happens to be the one to operate the machine.

We should say that there is a difference in interpretation of the word *clearly*. Cultural difference of each country decides on the standard of clarity, and it basically comes to nothing other than a difference of values. From these facts, we can conclude that the scope of work in Japan is more approximate than it is for American and British workers.

Do you keep strictly to the scope of work? An interesting fact is that nearly 80% of the Japanese workers answered "yes" to this question; whereas a little over 60% of the workers in T. Company in England answered "no." In general, American and British workers think of the scope of work as flexible, not specified. The Japanese workers, on the contrary, think it is specified and that they must stick to it. And yet, an actual comparison of job descriptions between these countries shows a great discrepancy.

It is significant that British workers think it flexible and American workers think that they have to work at various other things in an actual situation. The finding below points this out, too.

We have mentioned previously that Professor Cole claims that American workers are just as good as Japanese workers. He bases his argument on the surveys he conducted in Yokohama and Detroit.[2] "How often do you work harder than your employer or supervisor requires?" was one question. On a scale of 0–9, 0 being the negative extreme and 9 being the positive extreme, workers in Detroit scored an average of 5.6 points, and those in Yokohama 5.23 points. However, these points are derived in combination with the responses to the following questions: "How often do you get so wrapped up in your work that you lose track of time?" and "How often do you spend some time thinking of ways you can do your job better?"

American workers are conscious of work not described in the job description; conversely, Japanese workers are conscious of keeping rigorously within their scope of work. Probably, Professor Cole's survey reflected their different attitudes. It seems to me that his basis for argument is only attitudes of workers in Yokohama and Detroit. Standards of values differ from country to country. Let me call attention to this point: There is a great difference between reality and attitude.

If you go beyond the scope of work, what is it? This open-ended question reveals clearly the difference in the yardstick. When measured against the Japanese yardstick, the result reverses itself. We can find some that come under "more than employer or supervisor demand" by the Japanese standard among the responses in the United States and Britain, but a good many of them do not. Here is an enumeration of jobs cited as outside of their scope of work in W. Company in the United States:

Helping those who are behind schedule

Giving help to others on the assembly line

Operating the machine not in charge

Packing

Cleaning the other section

Opening the box for female workers

Giving help to other sections

Inspection or repair of machines

Cleaning one's place of duty

Putting back the scattered tools where they belong

Conveying things by forklift

Answering the telephone

Handing over to the next shift and assisting

Setting switches

So it goes. In the first half you will find those which will be classified as "outside of the scope of work" according to the Japanese standard. But from "Inspection or repair of machines" on, it has a look of customary procedure or course of action, not more than the expectation of the employer or superiors. Most of what is listed here is thought to be within the scope of work in Japan. The workers at W. Company think of inspection or repair of machines as being within the scope of the maintenance section even though they use the machine themselves. As a consequence, they put it down as an item outside of their scope of work. We asked them further what inspection or repair of machines specifically means. They replied as follows: retightening bolts, oiling after disassembling the machines, and so on. These are the kinds of things they could possibly do by themselves, it seems.

Responses from the Japanese workers were clear-cut. Almost none of those items quoted by the American workers were found. Most of the responses consisted of lending help to other shifts—that is, Japanese workers are conscious of others' jobs as those that concern other shifts. The kind of job that fell within the scope of work, for example, is "handing over to the next shift" (this was outside the scope of work for Americans). I must say that Professor Cole's conclusion only covered their attitude and is quite unlike what really exists.

JAPANESE MOTHERS AND AMERICAN MOTHERS

Once the phrase "We climb the mountain because it is there" was a fad. Can it be "We work because the work is there"? It sounds peculiar because here the "mountain" decides mountain-climbing and the "work" decides what is to be done, instead of people deciding what to do. Personnel managers in the United States always list the same problems concerning young workers as follows: They are simply "out of it," whether the telephone rings, or things to be packed are piled high, or there are parts to be fetched. They call this attitude of the youth "tardiness." We hardly ever come across this in Japan. Nothing ever is more different from Japan than the tardiness or slackness or being "out of it" in the United States or England.

In some degree, to be sure, the amount of work, not the worker's will, partakes in deciding his attitude toward work or willingness in Japan. American and British workers do not tackle work even if it is mountain-high. It even leads me to think, in this sense, that Japanese workers lack independence. It strikes me funny that a certain situation (that there is work is one case of it) draws workers toward decision-making.

A detailed study on the scope of work so far seems to uncover an essential difference between Japan and the United States and England. In America and England, the benefits of a decision-maker come first before an act, say, as a volunteer, or willing acts. They act as a volunteer once in a while, but we should not forget that what they do of their own will and their independence is not lost to the end.

The same is not true with the Japanese. Situation coerces him to make a decision before the benefit of a decision-maker. The independence is with the work and not with man, that is. No other explanation except cultural difference seems feasible. Well, then, how was this cultural difference brought about? Has it been inherited among the Japanese youth today? This is a matter that calls for our consideration.

A study by Dr. William Caudill and others of the National Institute of Mental Health in America helps to account for this decision-making mechanism. Dr. Caudill has added some comments to his study, which we think are very important and will quote at some length:[3]

Earlier studies by ourselves and others in Japan and America have indicated meaningful cultural differences in values, interpersonal relations, and personality characteristics. On the basis of this previous work we predicted that our Japanese mothers would spend more time with their infants, would emphasize physical contact over verbal interaction, and would have as a goal a passive and contented baby. We predicted that our American mothers would spend less time with their infants, would emphasize verbal interaction rather than physical contact, and would have as a goal an active and self-assertive baby. Underlying these predictions is the assumption that much cultural learning takes place out of the awareness of the participants, and although the Japanese mother does not consciously teach her infant specifically to become a Japanese baby, nor does the American mother specifically teach her infant to become an American baby, such a process does take place. We, therefore, also expected that by three to four months of age, infants in the two cultures would behave differently in certain important ways.

Our hypotheses were generally confirmed, although there were some surprises, and we conclude that, largely because of different patterns of interaction with their mothers in the two countries, infants have learned to behave in different and culturally appropriate ways by three to four months of age.

Moreover, these differences in infant behavior are in line with preferred patterns of social interaction at later ages as the child grows to be an adult in Japan and America.

According to the study, large differences between the babies' behavior in the two countries were observed. More important, Japanese babies whimper a lot, whereas American babies do not. It is a difference in child rearing, not inheritance, that brings out this difference in three- to four-month-old babies. The studies of the second and third generation Japanese-Americans support this. They are pure Japanese, yet, behavior of the third-generation babies is close to the behavior of other American babies, and they do not fuss or whine very much. The second-generation mothers reared the babies in the American way.

Taking these findings into account, we must say that a mother's attitude toward her baby teaches cultural patterns. The mother is a "cultural medium," so to speak, handing down patterns from generation to generation. If we find willingness only in Japan and no similar counterpart in other countries, it may be that this willingness is a cultural trait, handed down through the cultural medium, mother. If so, mothers' attitudes toward children hold a key to the investigation of willingness.

What, then, is the cultural behavior in Japan which the study by Dr. Caudill arrived at? Japanese babies certainly cry a lot, as if spoiled. It is somewhat subjective to try to distinguish whimpering from other types of crying, but usually our common sense helps us distinguish it from cries associated with anger or pain. In any case, Japanese babies do cry frequently. We can infer from this that they cry for their mothers more often than American babies do. Some other differences were noted. Japanese mothers stay close to their sleeping babies three times longer than American mothers. Adjusting the coverlet, pressing the corners of the coverlets for warmth, fanning the baby, and caretaking of all sorts are familiar scenes in Japan. Japanese mothers respond promptly to the baby's cry, wondering if the diaper is wet, if something is prickling it, if it is hungry, and so on. They also hold their babies quite often to make them happy again. More "skinship" is observed in them than in American mothers.

American mothers feed their babies according to feeding schedules. They scarcely respond to what is not scheduled no matter how much babies cry. They hold babies less often than Japanese mothers. They often talk to the babies and urge them to talk. To paraphrase Dr. Caudill, they raise babies so that they will assert themselves.

Dr. Caudill's study consisted basically of frequency observations of mother-child behaviors like holding and crying. It was not a study of consciousness of why the baby was held or left alone. This matter is left exclusively to conjecture by researchers. The cultural value of the behavior has been unmistakably transmitted through mothers, nonetheless. What is relevant to our discussion is what values the Japanese culture has and what psychological motivations mothers harbor when they engage in various mother-child relationships.

Some behaviors of Japanese and American mothers bear no significant cultural meaning, to be sure. It is simply a difference of custom that American babies sleep on their stomachs and Japanese babies on their backs. It is culturally meaningful that Japanese mothers respond more quickly to a baby's cry to take care of it; whereas American mothers respond slowly or take no action.

Mothers have an attitude of empathy toward children, and American mothers are no exception. They feel the sorrow of a child as their own. The desire to respond to it is strong among Japanese mothers but weak or nonexistent among American mothers. In spite of empathy, American mothers are keenly conscious of feeding schedules and their own schedules. Satisfying personal desires plays a central role in American mothers' lives. This is not as true among Japanese mothers. Any situation involving the child can spawn deep empathy. The chief characteristic is that it is a result of an external situation. The mother reacts to a "situation," as it were, a peculiar action which is not observed among American mothers. This reactionary behavior to a situation is quite different from instinctive behavior of animals. We can say that it is a cultural pattern based on the inherent feeling of empathy. Cultural behavior is an appropriate word to express this reactionary behavior to a situation, on which a rather high value is placed in Japanese culture. Mothers are required to give loving care to children. Indifferent mothers who do not give loving and tender care to children, indulge themselves, or go to work, leaving children under the care of somebody else, are held in low esteem. These values are now going through a transition, modified chiefly via American influence.

Nevertheless, children do internalize desirable behaviors which they learn from their mother's caretaking behaviors and values, and they socialize themselves as desirable social beings for their future adulthood, as Dr. Caudill suggests.

Willingness is a certain trait, which can be fully stimulated. Stimulus and motivation are part of expectancy theory which has been accepted widely in the United States: "much work yields much reward." Expectation for reward stimulates industrious behavior. This desire for reward, when boiled down, amounts to a desire for stability. Therefore, what the expectancy theory implies in essence is calculation. It is based on the belief that a person decides on a certain action according to a logical calculation.

This may be why Ruth Benedict analyzed the behaviors of Japanese mothers, basing it on expectancy theory.[4] She reasoned that Japanese mothers take good care of children in order to be taken care of when they become old. Her analysis is in all probability wrong. In fact, many critics in Japan have pointed this out.

Japanese mothers' behavior is based on desires that expectancy theory cannot fully explain. Can we not say it is because the underlying desire is unfamiliar to Americans? It is a reactionary behavior to a situation, with no goal setting or logical calculations. It is an act different in nature from "causing a person to do something via stimulating some desire," or "acting on calculation," which are the bases for expectancy theory. Willingness is instigated when a given desire, which people are born with, is stimulated. People are motivated to work when they derive benefits from it (when a reward is given), such as money or position. The stimuli here correspond to desire for money and desire for success, which respectively correspond to "stability desire" (desire to make life stable) and "respect desire" (desire to be respected by others) by Abraham Maslow.

Stimulating willingness, as expectancy theory states, is not applicable to Japanese mothers' behavior. Hers is strictly to be called reactionary behavior to a situation. The only possibility of action here is for a certain situation to exist. The situation, not including some corresponding reward, is not necessarily the one that pays well. It is somewhat like some money lying on the ground; someone picking it up is about the only result to be expected from it. It is the adoption of the situation.

The situation that *there is a lot of work to be done* is a cultural premise in understanding Japanese willingness. Stimulating workers can be done easily by putting up a notice on the board explaining the situation that a lot of work has to be done. It is basic for a Japanese worker to adopt the situation. He works because the work is there, just as he climbs the mountain because the mountain is there. Naturally he has other desires. So long as he is human, he is not without desires for stability, respect, self-assertion, etc., just like Americans. Certainly, creating a situation is not the one-and-only method of achieving reactions. Fundamental desire for adoption of situation is still rated high in Japanese culture. A person will be called a lazy bum if he absents himself regardless of whether he has a lot of work to do. If the train is out of service due to a strike, those who dare to walk to work are evaluated high. The same is true for those who are willing to work overtime. Thus, behavior based on the desire to adopt situation often has some overlap with self-sacrificing behaviors and assimilating behaviors. It is no doubt an act of self-sacrifice and an act of assimilation to the company to give up a holiday and to work overtime. But the

Figure 8. The Twofold Japanese System of Desire

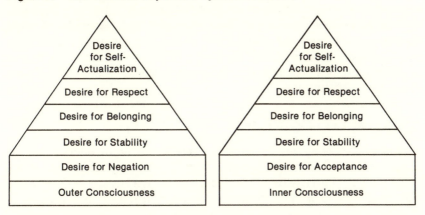

desire for assimilation is not quite identical with that of reacting to a situation.

The Japanese have desires other than those transmitted by mothers as a cultural medium. The Japanese and Americans have common desires—animal desires, as it were—for survival which is common to all mankind. But those which are developed later largely under the influence of culture are not necessarily common to mankind, though they are human desires. The fear of rejection typical to American culture cannot be denied in the Japanese. There is no denying, either, that Maslow's "need hierarchy" is pertinent to the Japanese. According to the values of the youth today, it is "desire for self-actualization" which ought to be distinct from the desires based on adoption.

I think the Japanese system of desires has a dual structure. The desires based on traditional culture, transmitted by mothers as a medium, have adoption as a base. Then come "desire for stability," "desire for belonging," "desire for respect," and "desire for sellf-actualization." Since it has adoption as its base, it is different from Maslow's system of desires. Maslow's system has rejection at its base. "Desire for stability," "desire for belonging," "desire for respect," and "desire for self-actualization" based on a rejection culture are in conformity with American values, and the Japanese have these desires, too. These are acquired through education and other social institutions, rather than through mothers, and are presumably fixed in what is called in psychology "outer consciousness." The desires that mother instills as a cultural medium are presumably fixed in "inner consciousness." The Japanese system of desire is twofold: One is rooted in inner consciousness, and the other in outer consciousness,[5] as depicted graphically in figure 8.

The values in the inner consciousness that have a basis in adoption have exerted much influence on will, patience, and the power of self-control, to be discussed later. They are related to selection of goals discussed by motivation theory and also to motivation theory that explains the Japanese psychology which posits no setting and selection of goals. I am quite positive that adoption precisely makes up the basis of Japanese willingness.

GO SLOW, LITTLE DOGIES

Reactionary behavior to situations, based on the evidence from the study by Caudill and others, stems from the mother's behavior. Mother's values in this case lie in identification with a child or assimilation. But these values of identification and assimilation are found not only in Japanese mothers but also in American mothers. Reaction to a child between the Japanese and American mothers being different, the use of the word *assimilation* is likely to lead to misunderstanding, however.

Assimilation in the case of American mothers is the assimilation with their independence secured or with values to keep their own benefit secured. It may be quite different from the Japanese idea of assimilation. Assimilation is often explained to be based on the desire to escape from loneliness. Here, the benefit of the subject of loneliness carries weight. But, then, it is an assimilation between subjects with different ideas toward each other, which goes against the nature of assimilation. From an American child's point of view, his interests are in opposition to his mother's. From a Japanese child's point of view, his mother's interests are an extension of his own. A reaction by the Japanese mother is self-sacrificing assimilation without the purpose of benefit; it is a reaction to a situation. As a result, the fundamental desire of a Japanese child is to be accepted by its mother. This is what I meant when I said previously that it has been fixed in inner consciousness. We can rightly call it "desire for adoption." Probably, the desire for adoption is not as strong in American children as it is in their Japanese counterparts.

In due course, desire for adoption among the Japanese acts as a propulsive force toward actions of strong assimilation in human relations, actions of self-sacrifice, actions of assiduity and moral training, and reactions to situations under certain conditions. We can observe as a significant common element in those behaviors that most work or human relations are "not of one's own choosing." The child cannot choose a mother of high status to be born to in this world; mother is merely "a given." Similarly the mother cannot choose to give birth to a future prime minister; the child is heaven's gift. They cannot make a choice based on logical calculations.

Japanese mothers' behavior in childhood fosters strong desire for adoption in the Japanese child, unlike the American child. Erik H. Erikson, an American psychologist, says that American children experience maternal rejection in their early life. American mothers need their own time and do not act self-sacrificially toward their children. Further, Erikson sees maternal rejection in cowboy songs—in the cowboy's lament that there is no way back and the cowboy will never see his mother again. The song goes, "Go slow, little dogies ... " The cowboy identifies himself with the dogie which left the mother behind when it first started roaming and sings that it is just like a cowboy, a long way from home. An American is like this cowboy, driving the cattle, all alone. He vanishes into the wild West, having been abandoned by the mother.[6]

In consequence, desire for adoption ranks above any other desire for a Japanese child. At the same time, reactional behavior to situations, self-sacrificing, and assimilating behaviors are input in the inner consciousness. I must say that the inclination for adoption for the Japanese is as strong as the inclination for independence for the Americans. Acts of self-sacrifice and assimilation for the Japanese, based on outer consciousness, however, go well with logical calculation in some respect. But reactional behavior to situations does not go well with calculation. It is in marked contrast to the action derived from the establishment of goals mentioned in the motivation theory of achievement. A comparison will further clarify the point. We might call it the reactionary behavior rather than the action based on some value. In this sense, reactionary behavior to situations is close to habitual behavior.

Assimilation has been explained as a psychological desire to avoid loneliness. It is a common desire of people to be united with the company, supervisors, and lovers, to be sure. In addition to this, Japanese workers' total dependence on the company, I think, forms the essence of willingness. The Japanese desire for assimilation, sprung from the desire to be accepted by the organization, is based on traditional cultural values.

Since Japanese assimilation has adoption as a base, it is not only an act of avoiding loneliness. Escape from loneliness goes well with calculation, but adoption does not. If we only think about assimilation as belonging in the outer consciousness, we will be caught in the same trap as Benedict. If assimilation to something other than company or lover is possible, it does not become an all-out dependence. An act of sacrifice in the outer consciousness, too, differs from an act in accordance with the desire for belonging without reward and expectation, which is based on adoption, because, in this case, the benefit from it comes first. It has often been pointed out that it is to some degree out of mother's egoism that she acts self-sacrificially. The criticism supposes the expectancy theory in the background, and it falls into the same trap as Benedict did when she thought that a Japanese mother acts self-sacrificially so that she will be taken care of by her child in her old age.

Japanese willingness, no doubt, is a result of all-out dependence on organization, assimilation into the organization. Company and self are united into one in the Japanese worker's mind, and the company's loss is his loss. His willingness turns into the company's profits and eventually into his profits. This is where Japanese workers differ fundamentally from American and British workers, on which I have spared no pages already. They have no desire other than the one based on adoption. What the Japanese have and what the Americans and English do not have is stability—belonging that has a base on the principle of adoption.

Desire for adoption has exceedingly strong hidden power in it, which often drives the Japanese to sacrificial acts. The very first action the Japanese corporations took in the recession due to the oil crisis was to give an allowance cut to the directorate on the management and to give a pay cut and a bonus cut to the executives. This is certainly an act of sacrifice. Workers took such sacrificial actions as giving up a holiday and working overtime without reward, wishing to be accepted by the organization they belonged to. We can say that one of the essential elements of willingness is an act of sacrifice founded on adoption.

I DON'T LIKE SUCH A CHILD!

The practice of permanent employment in Japan allows full expression of the desire for adoption. In a way, we might say that the practice of permanent employment in Japan is an extension of the Japanese desire for adoption. The organization is to the worker in this case somewhat like the mother is to the child. We do not come across any similar practice of permanent employment in foreign countries, since it seems so deeply rooted in the culture.

Psychologist Maslow made a claim as to the existence of a hierarchy of needs in human beings. The physiological and psychological needs of man form a hierarchy. He claims that man satisfies higher-order needs only after the lower-order needs are satisfied. The need for survival, to eat in order to live, belongs to the lowest order. This being satisfied, man does not strive for it anymore. The physiological needs are the same in every culture, but cultural differences are observed in psychological needs. Needs are related to human instinct, but there are those that are learned apart from instinct itself. The learned needs are what are developed later in life and are what Maslow calls the needs for respect and self-actualization. The need for respect from others may be equal to a need for status. Maslow placed the need for self-actualization, or enriching oneself, in the highest order. Naturally these needs exist among the Japanese; however, the need for success is not unanimously supported by the youth today. Self-actualization through work is not as popular as it used to be.

Needs for respect and self-actualization seem to be waning in more recent years, but need for stability and need for belonging in the lower order remain strong. We see that the need for stability expressed by securing a position in a large corporation, equivalent to Maslow's stability need, still has a strong grip on the youth. The need for stability is a manifestation of the desire for adoption for the Japanese, as we have seen before. The desire for stability in a Japanese is far more intense than that of an American cowboy.

Japanese desire for stability overlaps with the need for stability by Maslow, but not completely. Its foundation is not quite the same, as described previously. The desire for stability here presupposes human relations whose interests are not in opposition to the self, as in the mother-child relationship in Japan. This is the reason why they become wholly dependent on the company, and they showed determination not observed in America or Britain at the time of the recession after the oil crisis. I should add that a sense of crisis was added to the Japanese desire for adoption during the oil crisis. The recession made previously rebellious youths turn into gentle lambs.

In the United States and England, young workers must first bear the brunt of the strain caused by a recession. Yet, this does not bring about a change in their disposition. They have never known a mother who accepts them wholeheartedly, giving up her own pleasures. Both Americans and the English have need for stability, but theirs is not always the same in quality as that of the Japanese. They are inclined to turn to themselves for it; whereas the Japanese are inclined to turn to others for it, which is appropriately described by the desire for adoption. Somebody has to be there to accept them.

It is close to what Maslow called the need for belonging, if the term presupposes somebody to accept them. But Maslow's need for belonging and the need for adoption do not necessarily stem from the same source. Need for belonging can be rephrased as the need to be loved by somebody. In this sense, the existence of others is essential. But Maslow's need for belonging, which is American assimilation, seems to have some different aspects from the essence of the need for adoption we are discussing.

Let us take a married couple as an example. A large-scale survey is ineffective in finding out the nature of a spouse's need for belonging viewed by husband and wife respectively. We have to use case studies for such information, but there seems to be no comprehensive research,

Figure 9. Japanese Workers Give Paychecks to Their Wives

"Suppose you are a salaried worker and your wife stays home. Will
you hand over all your pay to your wife and have her manage it?"
(Percentages reflect "yes" answers.)

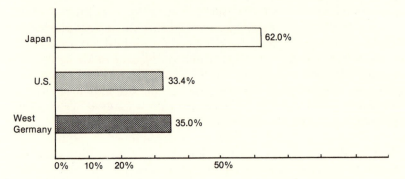

since the matter is a delicate one. According to our personal experiences, however, we often hear an American husband say the following:
"It is ridiculous to give money to a wife from whom one might be
divorced one of these days." A wife is often heard to say that it is
important to be prepared with a nest egg for the possibility of divorce,
so that she will not be financially strapped. Since generalizations from
a few cases often lead to a misconception, we cannot conclude that
these are common values.

Let us see if we can arrive at a general consideration. It may be out
of fashion these days, but in cases where only the husband earns an
income and the wife stays home, does the husband ever give his wife
his pay and have her manage it? Does he hand over all his income to
her? Is there any difference between Japan and the United States? If
the wife is entrusted with all the money, here would be a good chance
for her to save some secretly. If American husbands and wives are
conscious of a possible divorce, there would be a tendency for the husband not to entrust his pay to his wife.

Here is a survey on household management of money which asked
the following question: "Suppose you are a salaried worker and your
wife stays home. Will you hand over all your pay to your wife and have
her manage it?"[7]

Many young men in America and West Germany responded "no."
How about in Japan? Contrary to the United States and German re-
spondents, many young men in Japan answered in the affirmative.
Responses are summarized in figure 9.

The result, of course, is not proof of their consciousness of a possible divorce. However, it might help to conjecture as to what American husbands and wives at times express. It seems to me that they do not mention it only jokingly, so it is not groundless.

As money matters stand, need for belonging by Maslow seems to be a possibility when the interests of both parties agree. But can we think that it has something different in nature from the conception of adoption, "to efface oneself and accept the others"? We have other data on hand that examines this line of thinking.[8] It comes from an international attitudinal survey of primary-school children and their mothers on scolding methods (see figure 10). When mothers chide children in America, there is one taboo phrase, "I don't like such a child!" Mothers are never to say it. But why? They say that there is a fear of breaking up a parent-child relationship by mother's expressing a dislike for her child.

Dislike leads to being not wanted. It would mean divorce for a married couple. It would be an assumption of a possible break-up if "dislike" is a taboo word. There is a difference from the line of thinking that the ties of parent and child are there whether it is good or bad, whether you like it or not. Japanese desire for belonging means adoption, loving regardless of faults. We can see a difference here in the use of the same terms of need for belonging, although the need for belonging in the American sense is observed among the Japanese. The Japanese actually have two kinds of need for belonging.

The Japanese desire for belonging to the group of colleagues and superiors can best be described as a need for adoption, transcending time and likes and dislikes. It is a different kind of belonging from the one with a premise of a possible divorce. The Japanese will be placed under severe pressure if this belonging that transcends time and circumstances is endangered. It is more than they can bear to get a cold shoulder from colleagues in the daily workplace. I think that this desire for adoption is in a way what supports the group dynamics typical of the Japanese.

I have already mentioned the case where Nancy insisted on getting her bonus. The case seems to prove that the Japanese desire for adoption does not exist among the British.

TO HELL WITH WHAT OTHERS THINK

After all, the need for self-actualization is probably the one not satisfied on the shop floor. Maslow classified this need as being of the highest order. Young people today say that "they earnestly want to put themselves into what really satisfies them. To hell with what others think." "To hell with what others think" are the words that reveal their new values, and these are the very words that give concrete

Figure 10. How Japanese and American Mothers Scold Their Children

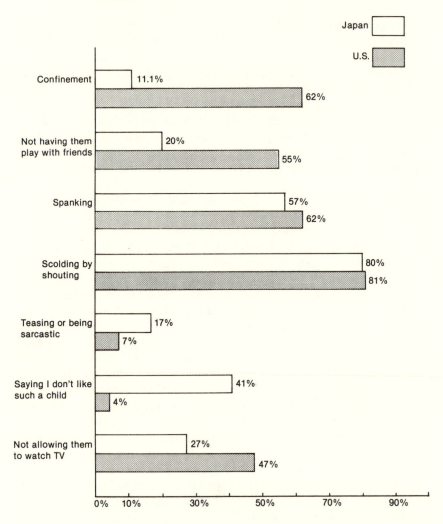

expression to the desire for self-actualization. How do they like the work on the actual shop floor? Repetition after repetition, the work is far from "interesting" or "irresistible." It is not an ideal way of pursuing self-actualization. They have truly good reason to say so. They are unfortunate, moreover, because they profess that the purpose of their working is *self-actualization*.

In a recent survey of youths, about 30% chose "self-actualization" over "income" and "social responsibility" as their purpose for working.

Further analysis showed that their principal reason for the choice of "income" is that "self cannot be actualized in work." It does not take long to conclude that all youths yearn for self-actualization.

What is self-actualization, then? It is, among other things, to realize what one wishes to accomplish. No one, for sure, wants to accomplish run-of-the-mill, routine work. Consequently, this desire for self-actualization could be an extremely important issue. This is why willingness comes into queston, but let us examine in more detail what self-actualization means to the Japanese.

There seems to be a slight discrepancy between working "because we have to" and "willingness" as used in our daily speech. The need for self-actualization, as Maslow posits, is the highest-order need of man and is the need that has cultural aroma. When man is hovering between life and death, his only desire is to live. After he regains his presence of mind, he wants to make his life stable. His life being stable, he desires to belong to organizations of people and to be loved by them. This being satisfied, he comes to have a higher need to be respected by others. He has need for respect such as entering a top-ranking college or becoming a section chief. When these needs are fulfilled, they no longer are the central concerns. He then devotes himself to what he really wants to accomplish. After securing a post in an organization and not being in need of money, the only strong desire left is to self-actualize. The need for self-actualization is different in nature from a "must do" attitude and close to "willing to do" or "irresistibly interesting to do," in fact quite opposite from the first. Willingness could be the desire to do "just as one pleases." I am positive that it is of a different quality.

Let us give thought to our daily work. Scarcely ever do we come across something irresistibly interesting. If the state of being irresistibly interesting is the only source of willingness, then to incite willingness, we must only slightly change the setup of a humdrum job or eliminate humdrum work altogether. All these schemes also act as incentives to self-actualization. It is one of the points that management must address. The first thing that comes to my mind when I think of the incentive mechanism of the need for self-actualization is the Volvo method in Sweden.[9]

Dr. Hans L. Zetterberg, a sociologist, gives a theoretical backdrop to the Volvo method. He points out in the report of an international project, "Jobs in the 1980's," as follows. At one time, there was a "farmer" in the mind of every worker. Today, the farmer no longer exists in his mind. The contemporary theme in the field of sociology is how to drive the farmer out of the factory and make the surroundings comfortable for the worker. He means to say that man comes to hold higher needs when minimum conditions for living or other needs of lower order are fulfilled. The farmer of bygone days was full of willingness in order to make a living which was a minimum requirement. A Swede, quite unlike an old-time farmer, cannot cope with monotonous farm work.

Dr. Zetterberg, further pushing his points, turns his penetrating eyes to various restrictions on workers in today's factory. He poses this question, "What is wrong with giving a call to one's family or sweetheart during work?" The need for self-actualization supports the idea of eliminating that which is disagreeable. By eliminating as many undesirables as possible, the environment for self-actualization is better prepared. Thus, willingness conveys the same meaning as "desire for easy work." Perhaps I am not the only one to suspect that something is wrong. There has to be an *element of accomplishment* like that of bearing hardships in order for this to be a persuasive enough argument. Self-actualization in the sense of accomplishing what one feels to be interesting is the underlying philosophy of Zetterberg's or the Volvo method in Sweden. This is the same as Maslow's self-actualization. My doubt remains, but, here, let me present what sounds like a typical example of self-actualization.

An American attorney had once been so engrossed in his work that he didn't know that the building was raging in flames. He was forcibly removed by firemen. His engrossment was some indication of his devotion to the work he was eager to accomplish. I can sense that he was either irresistibly interested in his work or foolish enough that a fire did not frighten him. His case seems to be a step closer to self-actualization than the Volvo method, in that he was accomplishing a difficult task. A further study will be necessary, though, to get at the real situation.

Absorbed as he was in his work, this American lawyer should not forget that he was in the way of the fire fighters. It is undesirable to ignore the trouble that one might be causing others. This type of person performs the work "he wishes to," but has a strong tendency not to perform the work "he has to," because he does not care about others. He will not cooperate with others, to start with, and has an acute weakness of not fitting into the bureaucratic organization. It may be self-actualization, to be sure, to do what is irresistibly interesting or to put oneself into what one wants to do, but it is too self-centered to call it willingness. It will not be real willingness without including other beings. Probably, nearly every Japanese will have doubts about the Volvo method or the American lawyer. It will be real willingness that dispels the doubt.

What is it, then? It seems as though the ability to be able to reconcile oneself with others and with situations is at the base of willingness. To throw oneself into such a situation and enlighten oneself is the key factor in true self-actualization.

TROUBLE OVER AWARDS FOR GOOD IDEAS

Mr. Lou, the personnel manager, was proud. He gave "freedom to think" to his employees. He received as many as twenty-five suggestions or proposals every month as a result. The company is happy with the profits they bring in, and the employees are happy with dividends, he says.

Of several hundred thousand companies in America, only a few (1,500) have been successful in adopting the proposal system. No wonder it is a success worth boasting about to get twenty-five proposals every month from 700 workers. The proposal system is as desirable for employees as it is for the company. There is no doubt about it. Undeniable is the fact that it has the significance of giving "freedom to think" to the employees, over which Mr. Lou takes pride. As was mentioned before, "thinking" is the business of management, not workers. At the base of it is the fact that management has little or no trust in the ability of the workers to think.

Management expects no thinking from workers, partially because they have concluded that it is of "no use for the workers to think." Hence, management gives practically no time for thinking. Therefore, it is possible for management to consider "bestowing" this "freedom to think."

Returning to our subject, there is no basis for self-actualization need without thinking. It could be possible to self-actualize if great patience were exercised while working a boring job for many years, but this is an exception. Some accomplishment constitutes self-actualization, but a free-thinking man is the essence of realizing it. This is where the satisfaction is found. The proposal system was considered successful with twenty-five proposals a month in S. Company where Mr. Lou works, but it is not the case with most American companies. Self-interest and short-range goals undermine the need for self-actualization. At W. Company in America, the proposal system was abolished soon after it was started. It was due to a problem that might cause a Japanese to say, "Something is really wrong with them." Anybody who could picture what actually happened, we would think, really knows American culture. Here is the story.

The first proposal was a rather splendid one. The company, especially the manager in charge of the proposal system, was greatly pleased. It was estimated that it increased profits by $10,000, and a prize of $500 (5% of the profits) was paid to the proposer. He was happy, too. The next proposal was no less splendid than the first one. The company enjoyed this run of good luck, thinking that the system was paying off. But their good luck quickly ran out. Lights are usually followed by shadows, as the proverb goes. When the company tried to pay $500 prize money to the second proposer, he flatly refused it.

Here is the proposer's side of the story. His proposal was bound to produce more profits than the first one. He was not satisfied receiving the same amount of money as the first proposer. He wanted to know precisely the amount of profit from both his and the previous proposal. It was quite hard to calculate exactly. One finds indefinite elements and things that are hard to evaluate. But it should have been calculated since the prize money had been based on 5% of the profits. At least, it is assumed that a calculation was possible. The proposer wanted to know it, and a response of "not calculable" was unacceptable.

Not satisfied with the response from the company, the second proposer took the matter to the union leader. The union sided with him, and the case was developing into a confrontation between management and labor. It was supposed to satisfy both, but now it was beginning to look like an all-out war between the two. Lengthy conferences went on for days. The amount of data prepared was as thick as a book, but the company could not convince the union. The war came to an end with a payment of $2,000 to the proposer.

What are we to learn from this confrontation? Of course, there is this difficulty of carrying through equality, but the fact that "freedom given" was changed to a sum of money is important. The company abolished the proposal system. Hourly workers are not required to think anymore.

A sense of self-actualization can come from discovering a new method or creating something. Americans failed because they attached monetary value to this phenomenon. It is probably because personal profit and satisfaction were placed above the need for self-actualization, which underlies the failure. As we have already seen, we found in Japanese mothers' behaviors a reaction to a situation or a sacrificial act or an act of moral training or self-discipline. I will call the last act of moral training or self-discipline an "act of devotion" for convenience. The American lawyer's fanaticism for work by braving a fire is a different type from W. Company's case of the proposals, in that money was not an urgent quest for the lawyer. It is the same, though, in that it comprises self-satisfaction. The basis of the need for self-actualization seems different from the Japanese basis, which becomes self-enlightenment or devotion. The American lawyer's act includes a factor for self-improvement and is quite sacrificial because he is not frightened by fire. But, still, it is essentially different from what a Japanese thinks as self-enlightenment.

We have survey data at hand on what the Japanese choose as self-improvement or self-enlightenment.[10] Surprisingly enough, as many as 100% of executives and 98.3% of workers chose "work itself," leaving reading or training far behind. Work itself is a stepping-stone for self-improvement. It belongs to a different level from doing things out of interest. It shows very well the frame of mind that the Japanese have toward work. We can say that something sacrificial or devotional to be adapted to a given situation is supporting the willingness.

To be sure, the act of self-actualization by the American lawyer and the act of devotion are similar. The two acts overlap. But we should make a distinction between the act of self-actualization and devotion. The objective of the American lawyer, like the proposal system of W. Company, places priority on satisfaction of self, not on situation.

Self-actualization according to Maslow does not include desire for devotion, a variation of desire for adoption. Desire for devotion is the desire to be important, controlling oneself under hardships. It is like the need for self-actualization in that what would otherwise be considered a hardship is not considered a hardship. But desire for devotion aims principally at becoming a fine man, whether one thinks of hardship as hardship or not; whereas need for self-actualization aims principally at finding satisfaction in being engrossed. It aims at being too interested to stop.

In the need for self-actualization, existence of one's concrete objective is placed first. Then, one uses his own power to create a situation in which to accomplish the objective. In desire for devotion, more weight is given to coping with a difficult situation rather than creating a situation for accomplishing an objective. "What one wishes to do" comes in the fore, in the case of self-actualization. For devotion, adjustment to a given situation becomes important, which may happen to be "what one does not wish to do" in certain circumstances, and one finds a meaning in self-improvement by so doing. Even if there is an obnoxious fellow at the office, a worker empties his heart and acts harmoniously with him. He tries to improve his personality by so doing. Desire for devotion is passive and a situation reaction type. Desire for self-actualization is active and a situation creation type. The difference between the two is whether there is a choice or not.

Desire for devotion has no end, since there is no stop to personality perfection. Desire for devotion does not involve satisfaction. When one is satisfied, the driving force then disappears, as outlined in Maslow's theory. Suppose one works for the desire for bread. One's willingness is gone once he finds himself provided with enough. The same is true for self-actualization. Work being completed and the goal achieved, one's driving force diminishes.

In the president's office of a knitted-goods wholesale firm in Osaka, I found a tablet with the following words on the wall.

Dictum for Merchants by Master Kazan

1. Get up earlier than servants in the morning.

2. Take better care of clients who can pay a hundred *mon* [poor] than those who can pay ten *ryo* [rich].

3. If a customer comes back dissatisfied with your goods, treat him with more courtesy than when you sell.

4. The more you prosper, be the more frugal.

5. Make a note of spending beginning with a *mon*.

6. Remember the time of the founding of the house.

7. If a house in the same line of business opens in the neighborhood, get well acquainted with them and encourage each other.

8. If you start a branch, provide them with food for three years.[11]

They all relate to self-cultivation rather than teach the knack of profit making. This is a case of self-enlightenment and can rightly be called devotion. The president of the wholesale firm is somebody who casually puts these ethics into action. He tries to be willingly responsible for what seems to be a tough piece of work. What is interesting is that business naturally thrives this way, he says. If one only chases after profits, customers as well as supporters desert you. Business starts with one's own betterment, according to him. For many years, Mr. S. has paid a visit to a shrine on the first of every month and does not work on that day. It is moral training for life, and I have been struck with admiration that the essence of Osaka merchants is as such. Shichihei Yamamoto explains brilliantly, in this context, about the cases of Mr. H. or Mr. T. in the bookbinding industry.[12] The workplace mentioned by him rather resembles an arena for moral culture.

What I call desire for devotion is still frequently observed in Japanese plants. Coming back to the proposals in Mr. Lou's company, the number of proposals in Japanese companies is drastically different from his. Besides, the ones in Japan are without the goals of reward as in the United States. Once Toyota had an estimated loss of 20 billion yen (about $833 million). But by making efficient use of proposals, they recovered as much as 16 billion yen.

In Yokohama factory of H. Manufacturing Company, they rank the proposers of suggestions much as in a sumo wrestling match. Grand champion of the East last year was Mr. Y., a warehouse clerk, with 191 proposals, and grand champion of the West came next with 104 proposals. The proposals of the two put together amount to a year's proposals at Chicago plant of Mr. Lou's company. I asked one grand champion, "Isn't it a torture to think up so many proposals?" He responded: "You can call it torture, yes, but going at it hammer and tongs adds to my own improvement. On top of that, it gives me much joy when they work out after so much thinking."

I said that the desire for devotion is a typical desire of the Japanese, rarely found in the United States and Britain. Whether natural or regrettable, this desire is steadily declining. Few youths work overtime willingly in every factory. Supervisors on the shop floor are agonized, caught between orders from the head office and the unwilling youths. Wringing their hands and hoping they ask, "Hey, Mr. so and so, is there any inconvenience today if I ask you to work overtime?" These days, many even add, "Let me treat you to dinner next."

Desire for devotion is obviously vanishing among the youth. They have only a slight desire for self-actualization. They say, "Let's give it a try since it sounds interesting," at best. Another problem is a disappearance of success-orientation among the youth. They are without the desire to be respected in the workplace, saying "What's the use?"

A major incentive for the desire for devotion is a situation where there is a lot of work to be done. Youths do not respond to this situation anymore. The situation where supervisors take the initiative and set examples is another incentive to the desire for devotion. The desire for devotion is the orientation to make a reaction to the situation where there is the mind of others or work to be done. An applied practical philosophy of the desire for devotion is taking the incentive and setting an example. The youth today do not react to such conditions. In other words, they do not possess the desire for devotion. There seems to be a waning of the Japanese desire.

FINE YOUNG MAN! YOU HAVE DONE ONE GOOD DEED

When we think about willingness, we cannot overlook what David C. McClelland calls *motivation for achievement*. Maslow's need-hierarchy theory leaves much to be desired. It is acceptable to use need hierarchy to explain the lower-order needs as in the case of hunger, but it is inadequate to explain man's far-reaching goals or endeavors over the long range. Talking about unfulfilled needs in view of far-reaching goals or endeavors over a long range lacks the consideration for stimulus.

There are two aspects we must consider when we think about how a man takes certain actions. We need to take into account what might be called *motivation for growth*, which sustains tension, as well as what Maslow thought of as tension due to lack of motivation which gets eased after it is satisfied. Nothing can explain the repetitious act on the shop floor except a "desire for maintaining tension." Motivation for achievement enters here, with the goal focused on maintaining tension and willingness.

McClelland explains motivation for achievement as motivation "concerning some kind of valuable goal such as the desire for successful accomplishment of a difficult task, or for better results than others via competition; it is the motivation to attain as much as possible by exerting one's power and overcoming difficulty."[13]

This motivation for achievement is surely a principle that applies in the Japanese factory. Some who lack self-confidence or who have a low achievement motivation establish unattainable goals, opening room for failure. Some only establish easily attainable goals. There has been a cry for the necessity of management-set objectives in Japan, too. There is reason to believe that goal-setting practices are behind this change.

We must think about the Japanese desire for adoption here. Establishing an objective of one's accord is not part of this desire for adoption. Rather, it is merely a reaction to a situation. An act based on a motivation to react to a situation is in direct contrast to achievement motivation which establishes objectives to be accomplished. Motivation for achievement stops once the objective is reached; whereas one continues to react to whatever situations exist. One is not personally responsible for the objective, such as in the American and British systems. Moreover, reaction to situation is without end, with an element of devotion, as discussed before.

Motivation for achievement is an indispensable element when we consider willingness. There is a gap between the objective to be achieved and the present condition. Recognition of it acts as an incentive to reduce the gap. Satisfaction acts as a reward for this motivation, which will continue to support daily productivity objectives.

However, it is hard to conceive of all operations as having objectives. Another problem is that an objective can be established for some work but may not be possible for all work. One reason for success of QC circles in Japan is a disregard for Deming's theory, which is based on full digestion of a given scope of work. The reason why Japanese products are superior to American products is that the goals of limited scope of work by Deming have been disregarded. The objective has remained simply "whatever the situation requires." No matter how minutely work may be subdivided or goals and responsibilities established, gaps still remain between phases. Japanese management fills these gaps. In other words, quality improvement takes place in the area where it is hardest to set objectives.

Demarcation lines and job descriptions are appropriate tools for objective administration and are good stimuli for motivating achievement. But at the same time, demarcation lines and job descriptions are one cause of the English and American malaise. Motivation for achievement by establishing goals is all very well, but reacting to work situations is another equally important variation of achievement motivation. It is of a different nature, though, for motivational incentives are usually toward objectives set by others.

Tolerance is another factor we should not forget in daily operation. It is the willpower, the self-control, or the patience needed to go through difficulties and to restrain other desires. Satisfying desires is essential when discussing willingness, such as the need for respect in that one can become a section chief, or the need for achievement in that one gets satisfaction from something. The Japanese have especially powerful desires based on the principle of adoption.

Recognition of those desires holds an important place, but it is the willpower to "stick it out" that carries the most weight. Satisfying needs alone has little bearing on repetitious, continuous, and routine work. Many youths say it is a good idea to be a section chief, but they refuse to be one if it takes so much doggedness. Extra wages or a position as section chief are not incentive enough. There is a tendency to leave those rewards of the game completely and not to work patiently toward them.

The following joke award in an American factory expresses beautifully the subtlety of this situation.

Certificate of Merit
The following is to give recognition for your outstanding work. Fine young man! You have done one good deed. If you do a thousand more, you will become a leader. Work overtime willingly and you will be allowed to explain all matters to the executives. You will be respected by everybody as a hero, on top of it. But this will not result in a raise. "Damn it."

Note: If, however, you say "Damn it" but once out of despair, all your good deeds in the past will be cancelled out and you will have to start all over again.

It may be the same in every country. It requires patience to accomplish work and maintain an endless effort. Incentives like possible leadership or respect as a hero have limits. Whatever stimulus you give to the motivation for achievement, it simply does not last forever.

One important aspect of willingness is the power of self-control and will of continuity, enhanced by a strong will. Where does this willpower originate? It will be the internalization of desire for devotion that exercises power over competing desires for idling or absence, etc. Given endless work, tremendous willpower is needed to draw satisfaction from it. Whatever the evaluation may be, I think we should take a new look at the unusual tolerance typical to Japanese culture. In this context, the need for self-actualization of "wanting to throw oneself into only what pleases him, to hell with what others think" tends to weaken willpower as well as it tends not to support tolerance.

CHILDREN CANNOT CHOOSE THEIR PARENTS
NOR CAN PARENTS CHOOSE THEIR CHILDREN

Reaction to situations may reveal a weakness in the egos of the Japanese. The prototype to reaction to situation can be found in the Japanese mother's behavior toward her child, where judgments on the matter are second to simply reacting to the situation.

Selection of alternatives via logical calculation does not form the foundation of reacting to situations, as previously discussed. This aspect is of extreme importance. Parents cannot choose to give birth to a future prime minister, as I have mentioned before. Neither can the children choose to be born to a father who is a prime minister. These situations are givens. The Japanese place great value on givens as if mother were given by heaven and as if children are heaven's gifts. I have varied evidence supporting the fact that Japanese mothers treat their children as heaven's gifts. This givenness is not confined to parent-child relationships; it spreads into many other human relations. This assumption of givenness is strongly observed among married couples.

Suppose one compares girl A with girl B as a marriage partner. One gets the idea that a decision is only a result of the fluctuation of feelings and not a choice based on logic. A Japanese proverb, "To a lover's eye, pockmarks look like dimples," is evidence that this is so. Yet, unlike Americans, the Japanese assume that marriage is a once-in-a-lifetime thing. It is because it has been given to them, from heaven. They assimilate each to the other, never sparing sacrificial acts. A Japanese husband acts strangely, in a way: he gives all his income to his wife, unlike American counterparts. He receives his spending money from her. We have to keep in mind that such an act is a result of a given, determined, fact, not a choice.

Relationships of this nature (parent-child and husband-wife) are carried into the human relationships found within an organization. One's organization is not the outcome of a logical choice for the Japanese, to begin with. Personnel staffs in an organization would find it hard to assert that they adopt men based on some logically calculated judgment of personal ability. They value whether a person can act in concert with others within the organization. A person gets assigned to his company as a given rather than as a choice. Though it may appear to be free choice, a mere fluctuation of emotion may be responsible for the final assignment.

Strong desire for adoption underlies loyalty to a given situation.

Childhood experience has been deeply ingrained in a man's subconscious, which asks for adoption intensely. As mother was a given, so were the organizations and human relations. An American renders devoted service of his own choice out of his own sense of responsibility. He shows no reaction to what is not his choice. If his chosen work specifies hours from eight to five, he will not work after five even if the situation calls for it; he has not chosen that. If he is a machine operator, repairing or maintenance is not the work of his choice. He will logically explain that lubricating the machine after unscrewing bolts is not his job, but is a maintenance job, even if it is the machine he uses.

He simplifies matters according to logical calculations and decides whether it is his choice or not. The Americans have no desire to be adopted by the organizations, nor do they have any desire to be welcomed into human relationships at the workplace. This is why very few take sacrificial behaviors in terms of human relations within the organizations and workplaces, and few try to assimilate to these work settings. Neither do they show reactions to situations out of personal choice.

Whenever attitudes concerning work are surveyed, the Japanese express a high degree of dissatisfaction. We can say that whether or not the work is their own choice affects their response. Americans always answer that they are satisfied with their work, while the Japanese almost always answer that they are dissatisfied with their work (concerning such questions as wages, human relations, welfare, etc.). The reason for this outcome is quite simple. An American entered into a contract with the work of his choice. It would be admitting his own mistake if he answers that he is dissatisfied. He is afraid the survey person will come after him, asking, "Why don't you quit and change your job?" He feels ashamed at his own response of "dissatisfaction," because it shows his own ambiguity.

A Japanese answers nonchalantly that he is dissatisfied because it is not of his own choice. There is no consciousness whatsoever of shame at this ambiguity. What is given naturally includes something unwanted. Nor does a response of dissatisfaction give rise to an attempt to seek another job. He still keeps striving and tackling what is given. He is in direct contrast to an American who will not strive and tackle what genuinely makes him dissatisfied.

I can say that Japanese corporations seek their prototype of organizational structure in the mother-child relationship in Japan. Neither management nor workers have chosen to form an organization. Both managers and workers wish to be accepted by a given company as their mother. Its essence lies in the fact that it is given, not chosen. This is the reason why they react to given work.

PART III

Generation That Awaits Directions

7

Egoistic Self-Actualization

IDLE AWAY OR SLEEP AWAY

What about those people who have too much money to spend? We envy them to no end; it is like a dream for us. What if man is so well situated that he no longer has to work in order to make a living? It is so far from reality that it may seem absurd to think about. But it seems rational to hypothesize, make an analysis, and get at the heart of the matter. Now back to the question. If you were so comfortably situated, which would you choose: to work as ever or to idle and sleep it away? It may be fun to ask yourself for your answer before we discuss related survey findings.

Perhaps a little explanation is in order as to why we asked such a wild question. When we think of the reasons why people work, there appear to be three major goals: One is to get income. Another is to find something satisfying and worthwhile in work. The other is to work for society and for the good of people, which presupposes a fundamental social nature in man. I would like to leave this last one out of consideration for the time being.[1] Our research team hypothesized that Japanese youths would say "work" and that American youths would say "no work," "idle away." Our guess was regrettably incorrect. More American youths than Japanese responded "work." It came as a big surprise to us. What is the matter with the Japanese youths? It was an important question for us. This was a good reason to take up the question of willingness in youths as an issue.

Let us proceed to further analyze this matter. First, we must have an accurate grasp of other survey findings of both the Japanese and American youths.[2] We asked the following question, "If you were rich enough to lead a comfortable life, would you rather idle away or would you like to be engaged in some sort of work?" (see figure 11).

In Japan, 24.3% answered idle away, in contrast to 14.4% in the United States. One out of four for the Japanese versus one out of seven for the Americans was a large intriguing difference. The people in the

Figure 11. Would You Work If You Were Rich?

"If you were rich enough to lead a comfortable life, would you rather idle away or would you like to be engaged in some sort of work?"

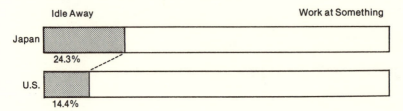

European Economic Community once called the Japanese "workaholics," and the Japanese have a long-established reputation as hardworking people. Many questions came to mind: What can it mean that so many youths want to "idle away their lives"? Is an attitudinal survey of this kind not credible enough? Should we question the premise itself of being rich enough not to work? How were the Japanese in the old days? Is this view of life a recent fad? We are discussing the youths, but is there any difference between those who are still in school versus those who work?

By answering these questions, we are relating the matter to the *yaruki* of the young Japanese. A bird's-eye view of it would go as follows: Values of the Japanese youth have been undergoing a drastic change in the past several years. They differ considerably from older generations. Workaholic may only be applicable to the first-decade-of-Showa generation, as it is often referred to. The differences within the American youths themselves become more obvious when we control for the variables: students and workers. American students are full of drive, while young working American youths are not. Japanese students, on the contrary, are not full of drive, while young working Japanese youths are. In accounting for this finding, the Japanese educational system seems to hold an important key. Those who are still going through education have a strong propensity to idle away their lives.

Japan has become a major economic power with high productivity, and studies on Japan are flourishing in both the United States and Europe. This does not give me a bad feeling. I become suspicious, though, when I hear them talk about learning from the Japanese. We must duly recognize the fact that the Americans and English have a completely different view of Japan. It is very well to have become a major economic power, but will the Japanese be happy in their private lives? They have become wealthy all right after working hard, even giving up paid holidays. This is all fine, but have they not confused goals with means? The French often make such comments, and the Americans and English seem to share the same feelings.

In a way it seems that the Japanese students anticipate this line of thinking. It is fine in its own way. The problem is that the Japanese youth have a deeper commitment to their attitudes than the American youth, and they are developing weaker senses of obligation. It may be a reaction against workaholism, but the swing toward idling away seems to be wide.

EXPRESSIONS OR INTENTIONS, THAT IS THE QUESTION

The findings to the question, "If you were rich enough to lead a comfortable life, would you rather idle away or work?" were made public in 1955 in the United States.[3] The results will be helpful in examining the present values of Japanese youth. A similar survey of the Japanese by NHK, a public broadcasting corporation, was conducted in 1968.[4]

First, let us look at the American findings. In 1955, 80% answered "work," and 20% "not work." When we compare these figures to the newer ones (from figure 11, 83.4% work, 14.4% not work), we can see that the young Americans of today are willing to work more than those of thirty years ago. The Japanese survey showed that 91% answered "work," 7% answered "not work" in 1968. Figure 12 compares these results with the youth of today, of whom only 75% answered "work." There is no doubt that there has been a significant decline in the willingness to work within the past decade.

Japan has become a major world economic power during these ten years, ingeniously overcoming the oil crisis, and has won the respect of the world. At the same time, more and more people are criticizing their overworking. It is of general interest, then, to see how social attitude has changed. The survey does indicate a great change within these ten years. What is significant is that the Japanese youth refuse to work, as far as their attitudinal expression goes, more than the American youth, who are said to be suffering from the American malaise.

Let us deal with possible interpretations of these findings. Attitudinal surveys mainly deal with the verbal attitudes, not necessarily with the true intentions. Or there is a related problem of attitudinal expression versus actual behavior.[5] Some people are critical of the attitudinal surveys, saying that they reflect only the attitudes and not the actual behavior. It is easy to be critical of the survey findings, saying that Japanese youth actually work so hard as to be called workaholics, regardless of attitude survey results. There is no truth to their

**Figure 12.   Decline in Number of Japanese Youths Who Prefer to
Work**

(Percentages reflect those who chose to work.)

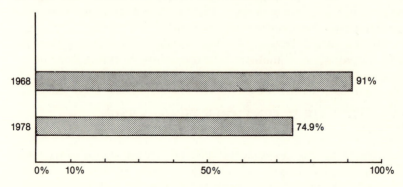

attitudinal expressions since their actions indicate other actual
intentions.

If a change takes place in the work behavior, it starts with change
in the workers' mental attitudes. Workers need reasons for working;
in short, mental attitudes precede execution. Change in attitudes gives
rise to change in behavior. The criticism that points out the discrepancy
between the attitude and behavior regards man as a machine, which
is wrong. The criticism lacks foresight because change is to occur before
long.

A man's attitude toward work, combined with those of his colleagues,
forms a social current. In this sense, we can call social attitude a current
that foretells where Japanese society is going. We also cannot forget
that youth are almost always the pioneers of social change. Therefore,
we must pay attention to the attitudes of the young.

Some time ago, everybody in the survey business talked about this
set of words: "X paper, Tokyo, college student." A person who reads X
paper out of three major dailies in Japan, who lives in Tokyo, and who
is a college student is to be the precursor of the time. Although arising
out of the intuition of the people in the survey business, it seems to
have some empirical basis. It is unmistakably those youths who have
been the leaders of leisure-orientation during the past ten years. Daniel
Yankelovich, an American sociologist, established that social change
begins with students, spreads over the young in general, then gets
firmly fixed as social values.[6] The youth who say, "I would idle away
if I did not have to work," are ahead of their time. We cannot dismiss
all of these things and simply proclaim that they are actually
workaholics.

How does the discrepancy between the attitudinal expression and actual behavior relate to social change? The assertion goes that the findings of the attitudinal survey are nothing but the expression of attitude. It is based on the premise that the expression of the attitude may be false, while actual intention is true. It is hard to tell whether the answer to the question represents expression or intention. It appears to be an actual intention. There is a trend in America and Europe to regard working as not good at all. At one time, Protestantism gave encouragement to working. The spirit is still there. However, compared with the Japanese, Americans and Europeans want earlier retirement, and especially in France, there is a strong preference for a leisurely existance.

Each society shares some common values. If a person holds certain personal intentions and has other competing attitudinal expressions, all differing from those held by society, he is likely to follow the generally accepted "expressed attitudes." This perhaps seems fabricated, but it is required, all the same, to suppress actual intentions and act in accordance with attitudinal expressions. It is looking at the matter from an individual level to say that intention is true and attitudinal expression is false. On the level of social order or the social man, expressed attitude is true. To the extent that man is a creation of a society, we cannot disregard the attitudinal expression. We cannot tell whether idling away is actual intention or attitudinal expression. We will not make it an issue here, since the matter falls largely on the individual level. However, we must pay serious attention to attitudinal expression as a form of social awareness.

The case of working in spite of being rich enough to make a comfortable life may be attitudinal expression. We have come to realize that we cannot disregard it as being only expressions. The fact that there was a decline in the attitudinal expression within a decade or so suggests that the current of social awareness in Japan has started in the direction of "not working." On the contrary, "working" is an unchanged absolute in the United States. Willingness is likely to become shaky in Japan, where working is generally encouraged as a social value.

COLLEGE GRADUATE FEMALE WORKERS: THEIR REALITY

At what moment do the youths find a reason for living? Two surveys on the life goals of youth were conducted. The 1972 survey was conducted in eleven countries including Japan. The 1975 survey covered only the youth in Japan. Both of these surveys were conducted by the Prime Minister's Office, Youth Bureau.[7] In the worldwide survey of the attitudes of the youth in 1972, the question was simply, "What is the goal of your life?" Youths in Japan chose "rewarding work" more often than youths in any other country:

The goal of life is rewarding work.

Japan	28.0%
United States	8.9%
England	13.3%
France	8.8%

We came across an interesting fact that in 1972 more Japanese than French claimed that "work is a reason for living." What were the figures in 1975? "Rewarding job group" dropped to 16.1% in Japan, a rather sharp decline. The figure for the same question in a similar survey nine years before was 30.4%. It was clear that a dramatic change had taken place in the five or six years since 1970. A tendency of leaving work behind, putting leisure-orientation first has overtaken youth since then. In fact, the "rewarding job group" declined from one person in three to one in six. This change coincides with the rapid growth of the Japanese economy. We can conjecture that as affluence increases, the economic significance of work decreases.

During the period of rapid economic growth in Japan, jobs were everywhere so long as one wanted to work. Some youths earned high wages through hard labor, hired out on a daily basis a few days a week. They spent most of their time just as they pleased. It was not necessary to find a permanent job. Daily-hire wages were quite good. Struck by the oil crisis, the young who had played the free-lancer had to take their old school uniforms out of the closet or get a haircut and find jobs.[8] Yes, they assumed a new profile, but it did not mean that they had shed their old way of life completely. Subsequent research and surveys indicate precisely this trend away from work and toward leisure, which coincided with the rapid growth of the Japanese economy. That's why we asked the question, "Will you work in case you do not have to work in order to make a living?" Meaning of work has three aspects as we have seen before. First is maintaining a livelihood (income), second is social responsibility (contribution to others), and third is fulfilling a calling (self-actualization).

Because it is clear that everybody is working in order to make a living, it is hard to choose which of the three is stronger and doing so may even lead to a contradiction. The economic aspect of work is essential to everybody. What is to be questioned may be merely a degree of necessity. This is precisely the reason why we asked whether one still works even when there is no need to, attempting to exclude the economic factor of work. This way, we get a sharper picture of the meaning of work. Maintaining a living is not the only meaning of work. A gambler cannot puff his chest and say that he is engaged in gambling for a living, because gambling lacks social contribution or fulfillment of social responsibility. Fulfillment of social responsibility plays an important part in work. Another important factor is self-actualization, which we will discuss next. People want to be engaged in some kind of work even if they do not have to work to live. It is because they have the objective of realizing their desire for creation or of having meaningful relationships with others by means of work.

We will next go into detailed analysis of "what people work for." Although differing slightly, the second attitudinal survey of the world youth asked about the important factors in choosing jobs. The following are the alternatives:

1. Occupation with much income
2. Occupation that can win fame
3. Occupation that is useful to society
4. Occupation with short work hours
5. Occupation that makes use of individuality or ability
6. Occupation that is stable

"Occupation that makes use of individuality or ability" received the most support worldwide. In Japan, 66.4% of the youth chose the item. Figure 13 shows the responses in three countries, Japan, the United States, and England. Hardly any difference is observed among the three countries. Here I want to stress the fact that the Japanese youth seek the same expression of individuality and ability in work as the American and English youth.

The response of idling away with enough financial resource shows a tendency toward regarding work in terms of income. The response of working in spite of sufficient resources is the case of expression of individuality or ability; that is self-actualization.

Here, it seems to be a good idea to make an analysis of the idling-away group in order to get fully acquainted with the profile of the self-actualization group. Besides, as we have discussed before, those who meet the three conditions of "X paper, Tokyo, and college student" are ahead of their time. We always find a vanguard group in any age. What is the idling-away group like? Let us go into details and illustrate the differences in figure 14.

"Idle away" is observed mostly among students, and "work" mostly among young workers. We noted before that work values in Japan are tapering off. It was students who were taking the lead. Let us look at the figures, first, of "not work." Among the high school students in

Figure 13. What People Work For: Comparison of Three Countries, Japan, United States, and England

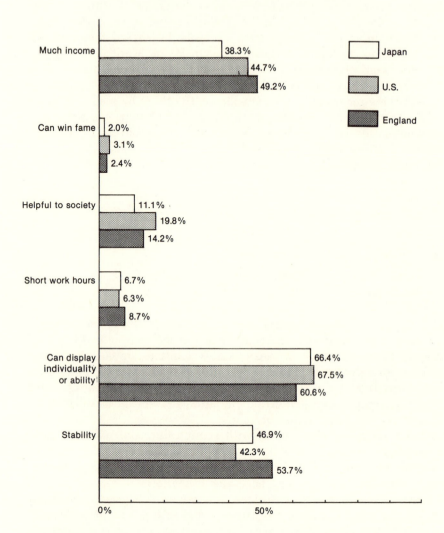

Japan, the figure was 27.3%. The figures for college students and young workers were 26.3% and 19.4%, respectively. Subjects in the survey are youths, ages seventeen to twenty-five. Young workers include college graduates who start working around twenty-two or twenty-three years of age. The majority, however, are high school graduates.

We must decide whether "idle away" or "work" is influenced by education. Therefore, it is important to clarify the attitudes of college

Figure 14. Comparison of Young American and Japanese Workers and Students: Which Ones Prefer to Work?

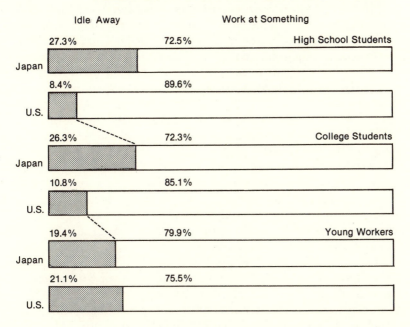

graduates toward work and the factors that influence their values. What do college graduates in Japan think about expression of their individuality and ability? A clue lies in what is considered important in choosing a job. Data from the three countries (now including England) were analyzed from several angles. An interesting finding was that the female college graduates in Japan were quite different from other female youths.

American and English female college graduates (especially American) base their selection on expression of ability and contribution to society. As newcomers to the work world, they are glowing with a sense of responsibility. It is natural on one's first job to wish to contribute to society and use one's ability. I was surprised that this tendency is stronger in female than in male college graduates. It appears that the females are free from falsehood.

Female college graduates in Japan take little notice of income and leisure. They definitely support expression of individuality and ability. In this regard they are similar to their American and English counterparts. Their genuineness and innocence are clear to us. We can easily follow their reasoning up to this point, but a further analysis reveals that they are far from being innocent. What is really on their minds? It is an intricate analysis, but it is a point of importance. Let us follow the data in detail.

One of the survey questions concerns dissatisfaction in occupational life. I must say that it is not easy at all to grasp the real picture of the female college graduates in Japan. They preferred self-actualization to income or leisure. They should naturally complain that they "cannot utilize their ability" in full. In fact, quite a number of male workers pointed it out. Female college graduates should voice even more complaints because they have a stronger inclination toward utilization of their ability than males. But this is not necessarily the case. It is unthinkable that female college graduates are given more chances to exert their ability on the actual job.

But, then, why do they not complain about it? It is a mystery, which puzzles me. There is a clue to why, nonetheless. Their way of giving a response to the question concerning dissatisfaction in terms of income and holiday is unusual. Many female clerical workers complain about low income and few holidays. But the female college graduates are inclined simply to choose "not applicable" in disproportionate numbers—that is, 30% chose "NA." What does this mean? One explanation is this: They have declared that they sought employment with a desire to use their abilities. They responded that income and leisure are not their main concern. But their real intention may have been different so that they could not complain about income, leisure, and holidays. Instead, they had to choose "NA." They insist on self-actualization, on the other hand. Am I guessing wrong to say that their actual complaint tends to concern income and hours more than self-actualization? To put it another way, income and hours mean money and leisure. They might have felt it a disgrace to put down money and leisure in place of self-actualization or expression of individuality and ability. They probably could not give a straightforward answer of money and leisure in terms of dissatisfaction about work.

This is the explanation that occurred to me. College graduates in Japan, especially female graduates, smack of something quite different from others. Female clerical workers expressed their ego candidly in all three countries, giving straightforward answers of money and leisure. Female college graduates did not express themselves, making no response. It is likely that female workers share similar concerns and interests although they have different modes of responding.

I am ready to admit that my explanation stems from my intuition, but college graduates who answered "idle away" have a different mentality from American students, especially American female college graduates. To me, theirs is mere selfishness. What self-actualization (or expression of individuality and ability) really means is achieving after enduring hardships and making efforts. But Japanese college graduates, especially female graduates, are simply insisting on their rights; it is self-actualization inclusive of selfishness.

TODAY'S YOUTH PUSH BACK PRESSURE

I asked Mr. Wright at C. Plant of W. Company in the United States: "What are you working for?" He said, "You know how a wife is? I want to buy this and that. She never holds her tongue. She keeps nagging at me the whole day if I don't go to work, saying that I get less wages. I never feel like relaxing at home even if I was away from work. I guess I am working because she nags at me."

He is the printer who prints askew on corrugated cardboard or prints only half of what is required. As a result, he had received two warnings and would lose his job with one more. His brilliant tactic was to ask the supervisor to lower his rank to an assistant. He used his brain as no ordinary person would when it comes to a scheme like this, yet he didn't use his brain to produce some device that would prevent uneven printing as his Japanese equivalent did.

I put this question to Wright: "Do you enjoy work?" He made no response. But Harv who was at his side responded for him. "We all enjoy working, yes, we do. Never grudgingly. Work is good. We must take pleasure in it." Wright, I noticed, had a hard time not to burst into a fit of laughter. All he had was a faint smile. It was precisely a sneer. Work is no fun for Wright. He is the last man to think of expressing individuality or ability in his work. Wright, this time, would surely break into a fit of laughter if I told him that work exists for self-education.

"What was on your mind the last time you were absent from work? Does the reaction of your family affect how you would behave?" We included family in the alternatives in the question we asked in Japan, the United States, and England because we had a feeling that pressure from wives exists, especially in the United States. As was expected, many in W. Company in the United States gave a response of "family" being predominantly on their mind. The figure for "family" is larger than the one for "wages." As figure 15 shows, pressure from family or wife is strong.

Japanese figures for wages, supervisors, and family are quite small, all less than 10%. But "work" on their minds is about the same percentage as "family" is in America. We might be able to say that an American is tied to his wife's apron strings, and a Japanese is tied to work itself. But when we look at the age difference among those who replied "work," the figure is lower for those in the younger generation. An interesting fact is that once work is off one's mind, one cares for almost nothing except perhaps co-workers. Japanese do not have to

Figure 15. Family Considerations Are Important to American Workers

"What was on your mind the last time you were absent from work?
Does the reaction of your family affect how you would behave?"
(Data from W. Company in the United States)

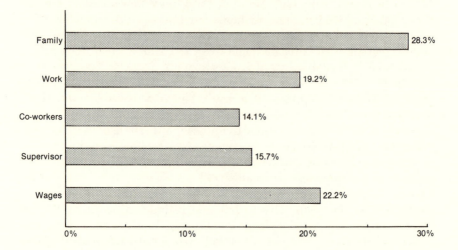

care about wages as Americans do. Thanks to the practice of lifetime employment, there is no fear of being fired or getting a wage-cut due to absence from work. In short, they do not get much pressure from supervisors.

As we have also seen, the Japanese willingness originates as a reaction to a situation. It seems that willingness loses its source once work is out of mind. In reply to the question of whether they would "work" or "idle away" if they were rich enough not to work, many Japanese students gave a reply of "idle away." Young workers, instead, showed a strong tendency to "work." The phenomenon was quite the contrary in the United States.

Probably, whether work was right in front of their eyes or not had an effect on the difference of responses between students and young workers. One big reason is found here. All the same, the current of willingness in reaction to situations is declining steadily.

We have also noted that college graduates anticipate the times or are ahead of the times and that their work goal is self-actualization. At the same time, the data pointed to an orientation toward money and leisure. Self-actualization along with money and leisure is an odd combination. It is a combination of American Wright and self-actualization. Wright as well as his wife aim at wages. In addition, he does not want to work. He is after money and leisure. It is simply beyond my understanding that self-actualization goes hand in hand with money and leisure. I find the combination odd, because self-actualization is such a lofty goal that money and leisure don't seem to be in the same class. Some of the value factors that self-actualization contains are such hard-to-achieve factors as effort and perseverance. The youth who says that he does not work provided that he has time and money is simply saying that he "wants to live at his ease" or he would only tackle something very interesting.

Desire for self-actualization has two aspects for the Japanese, as we have seen. One is what Maslow called self-actualization, which derives satisfaction out of accomplishing "something interesting." This desire is common to mankind, regardless of cultural background. The other is so-called desire for devotion, which is peculiar to the Japanese and which carries self-cultivation to perfection through work.

Can we not say that the values of idling away and those of expressing individuality and ability have a similar underlying base and that desire for devotion is missing from both of them? Yet, I doubt it to be the self-actualization described by Maslow. There seems to be too little self-restraint over other desires.

Let us look at it from the standpoint of motivation for achievement. No doubt, idling away and expression of individuality and ability come under motivation for achievement, which McClelland talked about. But reaction to situation, which is to make a reaction to the existing work and which characterizes the Japanese, is missing from it.

We can conclude that a new trend of the Japanese youth is on the level of desires and motivation for achievement and that the Japanese willingness factor is missing from them. What is more, what they call self-actualization is fairly dubious. What it amounts to is self-actualization of American students with self-restraint or duty removed.

There is another missing factor. As we have seen before, what constitutes work is mostly daily repetitive routine, and the willingness factor here is the willpower of self-restraint or patience that exercises power over desires for idling or refusing something difficult. This willpower is missing, too. I am afraid that the *yaruki* of the Japanese youth is approaching that of Wright at C. Plant of W. Company in the United States. I must say that this is a grave situation.

ELEGANT PHILOSOPHER, AMERICAN TARO

There seems to have been a split of evaluation concerning Darleg Toro. It was at C. Plant of W. Company in the United States. "That man doesn't like to take the responsibility. If the work gets heavier even a bit, he stays away from it. Doesn't he aspire for a job with a little responsibility, I wonder?" said the foreman, his immediate supervisor.

Toro is of Spanish descent from Colombia, South America. He speaks little English. The production manager had a lower opinion of him than the foreman: "What Toro hates is a night shift out of three shifts. He will be perfectly happy with a daytime job that pays him well enough. After all, he only hates a night shift. He doesn't want a promotion if it demands a little effort. He only makes it clearer than other guys."

Seven years ago Toro came to the United States from Colombia. He has a natural aptitude for the work but remains an assistant, never wanting to be operator. Night shift becomes a must if he is promoted to operator. Promotion does not have any appeal for him. He is often heard to say as follows: "Who is ever going to speak highly of me if I get promoted? Who is going to respect me? It is nothing much. What good is it if more work or a night shift are assigned to me with a promotion?"

Mr. Toro is thirty-one years old. He has a wife, five-year-old boy, and a girl two-and-one-half years old. They rent a four-room house. It takes fifteen minutes to commute to plant by car. He is always back home by 3:30 in the afternoon, and he spends the rest of his time watching television or playing tennis. His monthly wage is about 250,000 yen or $1,000. His major expenses are shown below.

Monthly Living Expenses of the Toros

Electricity	$30.00
Gas	$25.00
Food	$80.00
Water	$10.00
Transportation	$166.00
Rent	$250.00
Other	$50.00
Total	$611.00

Darleg Toro is an average American worker. We have named him American Taro because *Taro* in Japanese corresponds to Jack, a common American name. We asked American Taro: "Why don't you go for a little more responsible job and make more wages?" His answer: "You know what more responsibility means? More trouble. Wages are for my family to lead a comfortable life, right? We're comfortable, all right."

Toro's attitude is rather common in the United States. American Taro is just the right name for him. Is his attitude decisively different from that of a Japanese youth? One of our researchers posed this question. It is a relevant point: Japanese Taro is taking after American Taro. Work exists for fulfilling "desire for stability" and nothing else for Americn Taro. Desire for stability is to be able to lead an easy life. Mr. Toro was not keen on promotion. It is apparent in his statements: "Who is going to speak highly of me if I get promoted?" or "You only get more work assigned." He also lacks the desire for respect from others. His lack of the desire for self-actualization is similar to that of Mr. Wright whom we have discussed.

We posed another question to Toro: "If you think you have a comfortable life, you can take a few days off a week, can't you? Why don't you do that?" He replied, "You don't know the foreman? If I knock off too long, he shouts about a warning right away. I lose everything if they fire me. I don't want that."

All that works as incentive for American Taro is wages. The only motivation toward willingness seems to be the threat of firing if absent, since firing makes it impossible to earn wages. In American Taro's environment, there exists no mutual adoption among co-workers and supervisors which is the basis for Japanese needs. Consequently, it is not possible to motivate his willingness by contriving that absence causes a mutual inconvenience among co-workers and supervisors. Such inconveniences do not make him feel like running away or being left out. No reaction to situation exists. Neither is he motivated to improve himself through work. All these incentives are relevant in the Japanese culture.

What about the need or motivation maintained by Maslow and McClelland? As we have already seen, only desire for stability exists; both desires for respect and self-actualization mean nothing in work. From the standpoint of need for achievement, Mr. Wright, as we have noted, asked for his demotion just prior to his third warning. He took it to avoid being fired rather than reducing his junk-making.

Well, then, how does a Japanese youth behave in reality? To what degree is his behavior the same as or different from that of Mr. Wright or Mr. Toro? Let us start our final analysis by looking at the actual behavior of the youth.

THEY GO HOME WITHOUT STRIKING, EVEN WHEN THEY RAISE THE HAMMER

We often hear it said that youths today are not willing to work. What are the bases for this argument? Upon investigation, we learned of three phenomena used for the support of this argument.

1. They hurry home at the closing hour.
2. They do not assist others in their work.
3. They do no work unless directed.

Opinion is divided on whether the above three points lead to lack of willingness or not. Those who are in sympathy with the young say something to the following effect. It is reasonable enough for them to "hurry home when the time is up." Work hours are agreed upon from eight to five. It is an unjustified demand to ask them to stay longer at the workplace.

About "they do not assist others in their work," it is a mistake to go so far as to assist others in their work, since scope of work is defined at the outset. It is originally a mistake of management that A is occupied, but B is at leisure. They have made a mistake in allotting work such that one section is active and the other is not. It is the worst supervisor that puts his responsibility on the shelf and takes it out on B if he blames him for not assisting others when he has to blame himself for his own mistake.

It is an issue on the side of management that "they do not work unless directed." They should have functions and responsibility of work specified beforehand. Their negligence brings about the situation that requires directions. It is management without qualifications that puts their own responsibility of proper allotment of work on the shelf and then complains that "they do not work unless directed." In a word, they are *griping*, while showing their own stupidity. This counterargument is convincing enough. The points are reasonable in that they propose possible measures for consideration by management before they become alarmed about a decline of willingness.

Can it be, though, that this problem is cleared up if management takes the necessary measures? We need to know the opinion of those who question the attitude of the youth, not management, that they lack *yaruki*.

The first problem: It is a matter of course to hurry home when the time is up, but a closer look at the concrete workplace raises questions. I cannot make a sweeping statement, since work is different in nature from a plant to an office, to begin with. The fact that a typist stops typing in the middle of a word at 5:00 was a surprise to the Japanese of some time ago. In Yugoslavia, there is a proverb that goes, "They go home without striking, even when they raise the hammer." It is an ironical comment on workers who are only too mindful of their own interest. The idea therein will be that it is improper to give top priority to artificial marking-off of time when work is in continuity.

The civic life is affected by time limits, which is often called "red tape." Many people are dissatisfied with the situation that the window is closed at one minute past noon. They feel that a few minutes' extension will save waiting for the whole lunch hour. What is more, many companies are arguing whether 5:00 means the time to pass through a gate of the company or to punch a time clock. The loss is bound to be shifted somewhere or to someone.

The same problem is observed in the plant. Suppose one were holding a bolt in place with a nut when the 5:00 siren blew. If he hurries home with the bolt unscrewed, the bolt will eventually come off, making the product defective. He should screw that very bolt even if the siren blows. He should not leave the shop hurriedly even if the time is up.

In every Japanese organization, they have what is called *uchiage* party—an event to celebrate the end of a heavy project. They make do with a cupful of cold sake and dried cuttlefish, but the young are reluctant to join the party, saying that it is something extra not included in their scope of work. It is not merely a job-oriented get-together, since they are all fellow workers who have shared difficulties. Their conversation can turn to troubles they have gone through, thus bringing about a good understanding among them and agreement with one another to tackle the next worthy project. *Uchiage* party carries with it these functions, but it is very unpopular among the young. They play it cool and say, "Work is work. It is something you devote yourself to and do well." It might hinder them from accomplishing work of superior merit in the future.

The second problem: They do not assist others in their work. However minutely the work is mapped out, some end up being occupied and some are not. Whether it is his work or not, rendering assistance is only natural, especially when it is conducted as teamwork. It suddenly happens that A must make a large number of photocopies. He would have to work at it until 8:00 at night in order to finish it. His customer as well as his supervisor has to be kept waiting until then. It makes more sense, then, if B assists, and the two complete the work at 7:00. This argument assumes that work allotment is tentative.

The third problem: They do not work unless directed. Some do not report low stock. It is a clear case of having to place an order if they do, but they remain nonchalant without ordering. Once there was a case of overdrawing which turned out to be a big issue. A worker had written out a check when there was not enough money left in the account. The person in question had the nerve to make an excuse that he wrote out a check because he was told to and that he was not instructed to examine the balance before issuing a check. It is part of the duty of the person in charge of accounting to see to it that there is enough balance left.

What a shame that every detail has to be instructed is the conclusion.

Most of what is considered tactless in the Japanese tradition is exemplified in the above remarks. Some matters must not be laid aside as lacking tact. Not all daily routine has been allotted. There are sure to be some matters that simply require individual judgment. There might be cases in daily business which require no attention under normal conditions but which, nonetheless, need to be reported after questioning and judging their possible future importance. It sometimes proves a disadvantage to organizational objectives when a certain phase of work is left out unless instructed, although the allotted task is taken care of for the present.

A worker should carry out, therefore, even what is not instructed. He himself should also decide whether to work overtime or not. He is the one who can judge its eventual merit. These are the grounds of the criticisms in general that point to the lack of willingness of the youth. There is a point, just as there is a point to the counterargument. At any rate, we have to know that these three behaviors are actually observable among the younger generation.

What is the fundamental issue of this argument over willingness or *yaruki*? How are the analyses hitherto reorganized in light of the actual happenings? Let us dwell on these points.

WHAT FUTURE SUPERVISORS KEEP IN MIND

Hurrying home at the closing time.

No assisting others in their work.

No working unless directed.

The majority took these behaviors as supporting evidence that the younger generation lacks willingness. Others concluded that it was a problem of management, not the young. Where does their difference lie? As to the working manner of the young, one has formed a positive opinion, and the other a negative view from the same behaviors. They drew different conclusions from the same behavior because of their difference in appraisal. They each used a different yardstick, ending up with different conclusions. What sort of yardsticks did they use, then? A fundamental cause of this issue is found in the yardsticks.

Let us first scrutinize the yardstick that leads to a positive opinion. Their grounds for assertion at issue appear to be logically organized. Taking it up first will make the discussion easier to follow. Their yardstick goes with the values that place emphasis on the clear-cut scope of responsibility. One's scope of responsibility is from eight to five. Nothing could be wrong with hurrying home at 5:00. One's scope of duty has been made clear. Others have their own scope of duty. All one has to do is to keep his own scope well. Nothing is wrong with not assisting others in their work. Even if he is not instructed, his job has been specified, and all he has to do is stick to it. He could be instructed if necessary. It is a mistake of management to assume that they do not tackle something unless directed.

It is obvious that the grounds for this argument favor limits of responsibility. The conclusion is that the young are willing to work within a specified scope of duty. It now becomes unmistakably clear that their point of argument is based on a theory of individual responsibility of American management. Management theory by Taylor states precisely that individual scope of responsibility is to be determined and that job is to be divided as finely as possible. Deming, concerning QC circles, subscribes to this theory, too. He argues that complete control over scope of responsibility of each individual results in complete quality control. The odds seem to be against the argument that supports lack of willingness under the prevalence of American labor management. Their argument tends to concern human feelings or that of *naniwabushi* (traditional popular tales of justice and charity in Japan) rather than reasoning. Stemming from old Japanese stories, it does not seem to impress the young even when considered in a most favorable light. Let me argue whether it is truly *naniwabushi* without theoretical grounds.

When we look at it from a viewpoint of individual claim of the working youth, American labor management is well grounded. But the Japanese are possessed of needs and values which the Americans are not, as we have seen. There ought to be a Japanese yardstick instead of the one by Taylor. In fact, we can observe many behaviors not based on values of limitation in daily work activities of the Japanese.

This fact has become fairly obvious when we previously asked if workers helped others in their work and what it was if the answer was "yes." To the American worker, a small overhaul or lubrication of the machine he uses is helping others in their work, but it is not to a Japanese worker who performs practically all his daily work activities and probably the rest of his activities without basing them on a limited view of work. Substance of work is indisputably diffuse.

Diffused work activities are backed up by varied needs, motivations, and intentions based upon principle of adoption. The yardstick derived from them is actually that of diffusion, not that of limitation. Measured against the yardstick of diffusion, the youth are judged to lack willingness. They should not hurry home at 5:00. They should assist others in their work. They should be sensible enough to find what work to do without instructions.

We must turn our attention to the fact that use of such a yardstick is not limited to performance of work. Although the yardstick centers around work, it is also applied to human relations. For instance, people at government office windows should not be kept waiting as a result of setting limits on work time. In their life relations with superiors and fellow workers, they should assist them even if they are not directed, acting as a human being or as a Japanese, to use a more straightforward expression. These are just deeds according to this yardstick. Grounds for lack of willingness rest on, in the last analysis, lack of desire for devotion, lack of behavior in reaction to situations, and lack of patience. In my opinion, they lack Japanese qualities in particular.

Those who take the stand that the matter concerns management theory are constructing their argument on the Tayloristic management scheme. Accordingly, they do not question the lack of Japanese qualities. They do not expect such conduct from the start. They have used the American yardstick to measure Japanese behaviors to say that the matter has to do with management, not the youth. They are wrong. You have to use the Japanese yardstick to measure Japanese behaviors. If one is of the opinion that the American yardstick is right or it should be the one to be used, one should be aware of its limitations.

I think it is questionable whether the Japanese youth, as they are (in terms of money and leisure orientation and values that they would idle away if they had money), are accepted as affirmative, even if they are measured against the American yardstick. It is questionable whether Japanese youth follow the same behavior pattern as American youth.

American blue-collar workers particularly lack self-restraint among the American youths. American Taro was a typical case. Their response to the question asking what they would do if they were rich enough not to work is suggestive. What is to be a model work ethic in the United States is best revealed in the responses of American female college students. As we have seen before, their response was to work in order to contribute to society and to self-actualize themselves, even if they were rich enough not to have to. We should say that they anticipate should-be value or a basic principle of the American society.

What about the Japanese youths in this sense? College students who are ahead of their time, especially female college students who have been undergoing a radical change of values, direct their attention to money and leisure, rather than contribution to society. Self-actualization and justice appear to be what they advocate, as we have seen before.

Japanese youths in reality tend not to keep to their scope of responsibility which American management specifies. In a way they even lack an American sense of duty. It seems to me that lack of Japanese desires among the youths has brought about behaviors which fall short of some American values such as sense of duty, tolerance for hardships, and self-restraint.

There is no doubt that management improperly takes advantage of Japanese adoption for their business showings, achievements, or merits, which was allegorized as "race horses in the stable" in chapter 4. There is improper exercise of management authority, so to speak. Japanese organizations are steadily switching over to the American merit system. We often run into conflicts between the merit system and the system of community. This is not a case where a Japanese superior finds a good excuse to use his subordinates as tools for his own merits, in the American style, because of his desire for adoption.

The supervisor in the old days used to defend a mistake by his subordinate as his own. He even publicized his own merit as being his subordinate's. The subordinate responded to this consideration. The superior should respond to pure human love of his subordinates with Japanese adoption. A failure of his subordinates is his own responsibility as a member of a community bound together by a common fate, and his meritorious deed is his subordinate's meritorious deed as a member of the community. He should not saddle his subordinates with the responsibility for what he decides. In my opinion, these are some points that a future supervisor should attend to as a part of his duty.

Afterword

Willing Workers was published in part serially in a Japanese newspaper at the beginning of 1980. Part of it had been put into print a half year before publication of this book. To my regret, though, the person in charge of the column never allowed me to include analyses in it for want of space. It was an excusable reason, but, all the same, I was left as frustrated as ever.

Only a description of a fact might be more forceful than a poor analysis, in a way. Daily, we received opinions or reactions from readers on each article. Among others, many voices said, "Interesting," or "I feel the same way" about "race horses in the stable."

These are the words that Angela uttered in a loud voice at a meeting with employees of T. Company in England. Angela is but a young English girl. What in the world made her call the Japanese "race horses in the stable," and in such a loud voice?

The day's discussion had begun on a wild note, for Mr. Robertson took to attacking Japan from the very start. He said, "The Japanese work longer hours and receive less wages than we. It makes it possible to export goods at lower prices, etc., etc." It is true that such is an understanding of Japan by an average British worker, but a mistake is a mistake. I had to dispel his misunderstanding, explaining things one-by-one.

I went on to say that workers receive high wages in Japan; workers are highly educated; and they are engaged in brain work unlike the British workers. I added that there is no distinction between lavatories or dining rooms as in England and that their welfare facilities are superior.

It was at the mention of housing that Angela intervened. "I hear that people live in company dorms or housing in Japan. To me, they are like race horses in the stable, kept for races. They don't possess a single mind. They don't have freedom!"

Why did Angela's words evoke a strong response in Japan such as "Interesting," or "I feel the same way"? Were they delighted and gratified because Angela voiced their long pent-up feelings which they cannot voice even if they wanted to? Is it due to a masochism specific to the Japanese? The answer may be "yes." Their state of mind seems to be just like that of the Japanese when they were criticized as being workaholics. Somehow, the response seems to suggest a direction for Japan's future.

Interestingly enough, Mr. Thompson, shop steward, who was also at the meeting, was of a different opinion from Angela. Mr. Thompson, who was discreet enough not to raise his voice like Angela, said as follows: "Japan is exactly like a Communist society. I see no distinction between man and man. You do not find the same in the socialist countries in the past. What is more, you see love between man and man." To Mr. Thompson, Japan was all but an ideal society. Japan viewed by the English, and England viewed by the Japanese—it is easy to criticize each other. And the whole point is that they each "ask for the moon." Many of those Japanese who shared feelings with Angela cried for the moon—asked for what Japan lacks—and the same is true of Mr. Thompson. He asked for what England lacks.

Not long ago, Mr. Thompson sent me a picture of his family of four, himself, his wife, his son who is good at math, and his lovely daughter. Everybody puts on his or her best in the picture which was probably taken at a photo studio. A little artificial, it filled me with nostalgia. We, my family of five, had a picture taken in the drawing room with my mother in the center, who had just turned seventy-seven. We all sat on *zabutons*, Japanese cushions, looking in a manner Japanese. I sent it off to him, with an inscription of "Dear Mr. Thompson." A happy occasion of my mother's seventy-seventh birthday was a turning point for my children. They each left home and became independent. I owe the picture of my whole family to Mr. Thompson, for we may never get together again. Mr. Thompson said that it had been a long time since he had seen his parents who were living in Belgium. He was planning a trip south during the summer holidays and said he might drop by their place if possible. With a cold summer coming to a close, I do wonder if he made it.

The central theme of this book lies in what Mr. Thompson calls "love between man and man," and my point of argument is that this holds the key to willingness. Unlike Mr. Thompson or Angela, the Japanese possess desire for adoption deep in their souls. Desire for adoption has by natural process brought forth an employment structure of lifetime employment, dependency on organization, and a reactionary behavior to situation.

They agree with Angela strongly, on the other hand, on her opinion of their being "race horses in the stable" and wish to slip away from it. Aspiration for freedom or orientation for independence is widely

observed among young females. It is a rise of a new culture and doubtless will be passed on to offspring by young mothers. The deep desire
for adoption will suffer a change there. William Caudill showed in his
study that Japanese culture is anchored in a child by three months
after birth. Mother plays a role as cultural medium.

I have a feeling that the Japanese will run away from the stable.
They might even be running away at this moment. It is our wish to
show this cultural change after the fashion of Caudill in the near
future. It will be no easy job, since it is an attempt to catch a cultural
change. We made arrangements the other day to do this study at Red
Cross Hospital. We have been all overwhelmed with questions, and
the project remains as turbid as ever. It is my sincere wish that this
perplexity means a real start.

It is September 9, 1980, today, the "Day of Climbing a Height" in
China. It is only coincidence, but I worte the Afterword to a previous
book on September 9. Wang Wei, a poet in Tang, climbs a small hill
all alone in a foreign land and thinks about his far-off home country.
The ending of his poem entitled "September 9, Thinking of My Brothers
in Shang-Tung" goes, "When brothers carry dogwood up the mountain,
Each of them with a branch—and my branch is missing." These lines
cross my mind when fall comes. Each time, I feel like asking everybody
to climb a mountain together. I am likely to spend a busy fall again.

Now my manuscript writing is drawing to an end, which has been
a long ordeal. In writing *Willing Workers*, I am indebted to quite a few
people. Let me offer my heartfelt thanks to the people from corporations
that lent assistance to "Survey of Willingness" in the United States,
England, and Japan. I looked to Susumu Monma, the person in charge
of serial publication in the newspaper, for guidance; he even revised
my writing. I cannot thank him enough. I will make sure that he is
the first and foremost person to receive this volume. I owe everything
concerning editing and proofreading of this book to Jun Shibato, who
is in charge of editing in the Second Publishing Department of Art
and Science, Kodansha Publishing Company. Masako Nittame was
kind enough to read through the book and indicate obscure points; I
thank her for her patience. Last, I have to add that there are members
of the research team whom I challenged with my arguments whenever
my thoughts came to a deadlock. Sometimes it happened while walking, sometimes over eating, and sometimes in the car. The arguments
turned into the flesh and blood of this book, thanks to them. I am
reminiscing of those days.

Notes

PREFACE TO FIRST EDITION

1. The "Survey of Willingness" was commissioned to the Japan Youth Research Institute by the Prime Minister's Office. The survey was conducted from November 1979 to March 1980 and consisted of a questionnaire, observations, and interviews. The subjects were blue-collar workers from Japan, the United States, and England. The number of subjects was 3,549 from Japan, 506 from the United States, and 656 from England.

Three Japanese companies were surveyed: Rengo Co., capitalized at $26 million with 3,012 employees (number of subjects 2,947), produces corrugated cardboard; Hitachi Seisakusho, capitalized at $584 million with 74,942 employees (number of subjects 297), produces electrical machinery and appliances; and Hitachi Koki Co., in Mito City, capitalized at $18 million with 2,429 employees (number of subjects 305), produces electric tools for the home handyman.

The American companies, which did not consent to releasing their names for publication, were W. Company (60 subjects from the Modesto plant, 54 from the Atlanta plant, 72 from the San Pablo plant, and 12 from the McAllen plant), which produces corrugated cardboard; and S. Company (308 subjects from the Arkansas plant), which produces electric tools.

The English companies, which did not consent to releasing their names, were T. Company in New Market City (133 subjects), which produces corrugated cardboard; and Y. Company (523 subjects), which produces fasteners.

The author, Tamotsu Sengoku, the director of the Japan Youth Research Institute, was in charge of the surveys as a whole, with assistance from Herbert Pasin, dean of the Department of Sociology, Columbia University in the United States. Unless specified, the survey data used in this volume are taken from this survey.

2. Relationships of the people who have entered the company at the same period are emphasized in Japanese organizations where seniority is one of the key elements of promotional decisions. Personnel officers make an effort to treat the people who have entered the company at the same period equally in promotions or assignments. As to psychological implications of such a practice, especially in terms of motivation to work, see Kozo Nishida, *Nihonteki Keiei*

to Hatarakigai [Japanese management and willingness to work] (Tokyo, Nikkeishinsho, 1978).

CHAPTER 1. HOURLY WORKERS

1. As discussed throughout the book, there is a marked difference in work attitudes between the older generation and the younger. Some people see the difference in that, while the older generation worked willingly beyond what is stipulated in the job description, the younger workers tend to stick to what is written down as a justification for putting in less effort. Older managers observed that the younger generation work when instructed, otherwise not. Hence the expression the "generation that awaits directions."

2. The leading character in the TV drama was a junior high school teacher who devoted his life, private and public, with zeal to his students.

3. Arthur Hailey, *Wheels* (New York: Doubleday & Company, 1971), p. 12.

4. Japan has used its own system of naming year numbers since 645. Showa is the name we call the present era. The year 1986, for instance, is Showa 61. Those who were born in the first decade of Showa, therefore, were born between Showa 1 (1926) and Showa 10 (1935). This is the generation that shouldered the recovery and growth period after World War II.

5. A pusher is a railroad worker who literally pushes passengers into supercrowded railroad cars during the rush hours. They are often part-time workers or impromptu roles assumed by the regular workers. They are seen at terminal stations in the metropolitan areas, where many passengers change trains.

6. "Les Français dans l'entreprise" [The French in corporation], *L'Expansion*, February 1976, p. 65.

7. Keigo Okonogi, *The Age of Moratorium People* (Tokyo: Chukososho, 1978), p. 36. He argues that a legal word of moratorium is appropriate to the discussion of youth values today. There was an increase of students in Japan who do not want to graduate and find a job but would rather repeat the same year at school. They are thought to be avoiding paying their dues to society by delaying graduation. Thus the expression "moratorium people" was applied to this group of students.

8. Salaried workers in Japan are given about twenty days of paid vacation a year in addition to Sundays, twelve national holidays, and, if their company has adopted the five-day week, Saturdays.

The number of days of paid vacations depends on the length of service. Generally, it starts with seven days for the first year and increases by two days each year up to a maximum of twenty. Rate of use of vacation days is about 40% today, because the older generation often does not take all the paid vacations to which they are entitled as described in this book. The younger generation takes a paid holiday for granted, and their life-styles are influencing the older corporate employees. It has now become customary for most salaried workers to take a week-long vacation in summer, if they can adjust their work to make it possible.

9. Ronald Dore, *British Factory—Japanese Factory: The Origins of National Diversity in Industrial Relations* (Berkeley and Los Angeles: University of California Press, 1973), p. 26.

CHAPTER 2. MERITOCRACY

1. "Economy and Culture (14)," *The Asahi Shimbun*, June 27, 1980. Morning issue.

2. Leonard Silk, Economic scene, "The Slowdown in Productivity," *New York Times*, April 30, 1980.

3. Koya Azumi, Frank Hull, Jerald Hage, and Tamotsu Sengoku, *The Proposal to the National Science Foundation: "Technical-Market Context, Organizational Design, and Industrial Innovation"* (mimeo) (Newark, N.J.: Research Program for Innovation & Productivity Strategies, Rutgers University, 1979). The project was a comparative study of productivity and technical innovation in plants between Japan and the United States, to be conducted between 1980 and 1984. One hundred plants in New Jersey and fifty plants in Japan were selected for organizational research.

4. John H. Freeman, "Environment, Technology, and the Administrative Intensity of Manufacturing Organizations," *American Sociological Review* 38 (1973): 750–763.

5. Kenichi Odawara, "Dispute Over Labor Quality in Japan and the United States" *Keizaikyoshitsu* [Class on economy], *Nippon Keizai Shimbun* [Japan economic journal], July 9, 1980. Morning issue.

6. Telecast in Japan at 8 P.M., July 28, 1980, for fifty minutes by NHK as an NHK special. The original ninety-minute NBC telecast in the United States, shown in June, was edited to fifty minutes for the Japanese audience.

7. Most large Japanese corporations have on their premises a subsidized cafeteria where employees can have lunch at prices considerably lower than in outside restaurants. Some cafeterias offer a wide variety of dishes—Japanese, Chinese, and Western. The modest ones only offer snack food. In addition to being cheap, the cafeteria is convenient for those who are pressed for time and must take a quick lunch. Not only the rank-and-file but also the managers and executives use the same company cafeteria. Usually, a catering company operates the cafeteria under the company's supervision.

8. The "Follow-Up Survey of College Graduates" found that qualification orientation among government officials and achievement orientation among employees of private corporations are in vivid contrast. The survey, which actually consists of two surveys in 1976 and 1980, was conducted by the Japan Youth Research Institute. The subjects were, in Japan, the graduates of national and public universities and graduates of Waseda and Keio universities. In the United States, the subjects were graduates of Harvard University; and in Germany, the graduates were from University of Munich and Munich Institute of Technology. The number of subjects was 2,011 from Japan, 508 from the United States, and 122 from Germany. The survey was designed to clarify how college learning is related to occupational life and how graduates had adapted to workplaces by surveying them three years and seven years after graduation. Pattern classification by quantification Class III is performed to the data obtained through the questionnaires to the survey subjects. This is to classify holders of similar values, which resulted in producing two axes, one based on qualification, and the other on achievement orientations. For meth-

odological aspects of pattern classification, see Chikio Hayashi, ed., *Hikaku Nihonjinron* (Tokyo: Chukoshinsho, 1973).

9. Before the advent of electronic calculators, the abacus (*soroban*) was in the attaché case of the Japanese businessman as he traveled all over the world buying raw materials or selling manufactured goods. The abacus made the Japanese wizards at adding, subtracting, multiplying, and dividing figures of multiple digits. The assumption that the electronic calculator and computer have made the abacus a museum piece is challenged by the fact that, in 1981, there were more than 10,000 private *soroban* schools run mostly by individuals—an increase of more than 3,000 in five years. Hundreds of thousands of youngsters take the annual examinations to obtain the official *soroban* accounting certificate of the Japan Chambers of Commerce. Using the abacus is regarded as good not only for developing mathematical ability but also for general mental training.

10. Robert E. Cole, "Dispute Over Labor Quality in Japan and the United States" *Keizaikyoshitsu* [Class on economy], *Nippon Keizai Shimbun* [Japan economic journal], June 2, 1980. Morning issue.

11. Kenichi Odawara, "Dispute Over Labor Quality in Japan and the United States."

CHAPTER 3. FOREMAN

1. Studs Terkel, *Working* (New York: Avon Books, 1975), p. 221.

2. Ibid., p. 245.

3. Douglas McGregor, *The Human Side of Enterprise* (New York: McGraw-Hill, 1960), pp. 34, 47.

4. Ibid., pp. 47–48.

5. The original expression here in Japanese is *Katatataki*. It is a word dreaded by government employees who are past the age of fifty-five, the retirement age. The term simply means "a tap on the shoulder," but in civil service it has an ominous ring. A worker is approached gently by his superior—an actual physical tap on the shoulder may not take place—with a hint that it is about time to retire.

6. There is a fundamental difference between Japanese management, which is based on group responsibility, and American management, which is based on individual responsibility. Both principles of individual responsibility and group responsibility have a base in values rooted in traditional culture. Therefore, the difference is not to be discussed as a matter concerning only management technique. See for further discussion, Tamotsu Sengoku, "Nihonteki Keiei wa America dewa sodatanai" [Japanese management will not thrive in America], *Weekly Toyokeizai* No. 4185, Special issue, November 17, 1979, p. 118.

7. This is a Japanese proverb which means that "your behavior is enough to provoke a saint," or "there are limits to one's endurance."

CHAPTER 4. JAPANESE COMPANIES

1. Japanese corporations make it a practice to recruit workers regularly once a year in spring, the time when high schools and universities graduate

their students. The big corporations take in hundreds of graduates at the same time. The hiring policy is not necessarily based on the need to fill a vacancy or to employ people to undertake specific tasks. Because of lifetime employment and relative lack of mobility as its consequence, it is possible for the corporations to make long-term manpower strategy. Sometimes corporations do hire workers other than new graduates, in such cases as when a person with specialized know-how is suddenly needed due to expansion in business.

2. Refer to the "Survey of Willingness," note 1, Preface to First Edition.

3. Large Japanese companies maintain dormitories for their employees. They have multi-storied dormitories for bachelor employees whose family homes are far from the company location. Companies with many branches or facilities in various locations throughout the country maintain dormitories in each place to house employees transferred from another city. The use of dormitories is voluntary, and each company has its own regulations on the qualifications for occupancy. The communal dormitory life helps to generate affinity among the employees. The dormitory fee, usually a nominal sum, is deducted from the monthly pay. Some corporations provide independent housing for families.

4. Robert E. Cole, *Work, Mobility, and Participation: A Comparative Study of American and Japanese Industry* (Berkeley and Los Angeles: University of California Press, 1979), p. 242.

5. Working overtime is very common in Japanese companies, so much so that workers count upon receiving a certain amount of overtime pay regularly each month. This is particularly so among factory workers. Among young workers, an increasing number prefer more free time than overtime pay which is about 20% more than regular wages. Although overtime compensation is not paid to people in managerial positions, generally, from section chief level up, they remain behind after working hours more than anybody else—from a sense of responsibility or loyalty to the company, or desire to be noticed for promotion, or just for love of work. You will find a clue to account for their drive to work in this book.

6. Cole, *Work, Mobility*, p. 250.

7. Hiroshi Hazama, *British Society and Its Labor-Management Relations* (Tokyo: Nippon Rodo Kyokai, 1979). From survey findings, Hazama argues that, in England, confrontation between management and labor works to lower the productivity, while in Japan, labor-management cooperation enhances it. Hazama compares the latter relationship to that of a community in which everyone is bound together by common fate.

8. Ronald Dore, *British Factory—Japanese Factory: The Origins of National Diversity in Industrial Relations* (Berkeley and Los Angeles: University of California Press, 1973), p. 204.

9. Refer to note 5, chapter 3.

10. Bob Tanarkin with Lisa Gross, "Starting Over in Chicago," *Forbes*, April 28, 1980, pp. 74–86.

CHAPTER 5. WILLINGNESS AND ANXIETY

1. Refer to note 8, chapter 1.

2. Taijiro Hayasaka, Yuichi Yamada, and Takao Sofue, *Shokubaseinen no*

Shinrigaku [Psychology of working youth] (Tokyo: Yuhikaku, 1981), pp. 1–30. Adaptation of the young people to the workplace is discussed by psychologists. It is a matter of consequence in Japan that a worker is one with his superior and colleagues. This causes quite a few disturbances due to maladjustment to the workplace. According to the authors, the troubles and worries of this nature are common.

3. Robert E. Cole, "Dispute Over Labor Quality in Japan and the United States" *Keizaikyoshitsu* [Class on economy] *The Nippon Keizai Shimbun* [Japan economic journal] June 2, 1980. Morning issue.

4. "Stunning Turnaround at Tarrytown: Workers and Bosses Cooperate to Boost Productivity," *Time* May 5, 1980, p. 87.

5. William M. Carley, "Nuts and Bolts Issue, Closing of a Ford Plant Reflects Rising Worry of Car Makers," *The Wall Street Journal*, June 16, 1980.

6. Shichihei Yamamoto, *Nihon Shihonshugi no Seishin* [The spirit of Japanese capitalism] (Tokyo: Kobunsha, 1979), p. 37.

7. Ibid., p. 48.

8. Kozo Nishida, *Nihonteki Keiei to Hatarakigai* [Japanese management and willingness to work] (Tokyo: Nikkeishinsho, 1978). Nishida provides an excellent overview of the willingness to work of the Japanese.

CHAPTER 6. ACCEPTANCE AND REJECTION

1. Located about two miles north of Ginza, center of Tokyo, Akihabara is a booming bazaar of electrical goods of all kinds. Customers, for instance, can buy almost any type of vacuum cleaner, video-cassette recorder, refrigerator, radio, or home computer at wholesale prices. Also, at one store can be found 205 varieties of stereo headphones, 100 different color TV sets, and 75 kinds of record turntables.

2. Robert E. Cole, *Work, Mobility, and Participation: A Comparative Study of American and Japanese Industry* (Berkeley and Los Angeles: University of California Press, 1979), p. 234. Also note 3, chapter 5.

3. William A. Caudill and Helen Weinstein, "Maternal Care and Infant Behavior in Japan and America," *Psychiatry* (February 1969) 12–13. William A. Caudill and Carmi Schooler, "Child Behavior and Child Rearing in Japan and the United States: An Interim Report," *The Journal of Nervous and Mental Disease* 157 (November 1973): 323–338. From observations of mothers' behavior, the authors state that interdependency between Japanese mother and child is stronger. It is my contention that the same interdependency exists between management (mother) and employee (child) in Japan. Japanese corporations protect and foster employees like a mother, and employees depend on them.

4. Ruth Benedict, *The Chrysanthemum and the Sword: Patterns of Japanese Culture* (Boston: Houghton Mifflin Company, 1946), p. 101.

5. Tamotsu Sengoku, *Hikaku Sararimanron* [Comparative study of salaried workers] (Tokyo: Toyokeizaishiposha, 1977), p. 42. Based on the "Follow-Up Survey of College Graduates" (refer to note 8, chapter 2), I have argued that, in Japan, corporations do not employ specialists but train their employees to be generalists. Whereas in the United States and Germany, corporations hire college graduates as specialists. The existence of lifetime employment practice

in Japan makes a crucial difference. In Japan, employees are not put to work until they complete a several-month to one-year training session after employment. In colleges, therefore, students are encouraged and educated to be men of common sense rather than professionals, as a matter of emphasis.

6. Erik H. Erikson, *Childhood and Society* (New York: W. W. Norton and Company, 1963), pp. 288, 303–304.

7. "Survey of Social Model" by the Prime Minister's office, Youth Bureau, in March 1975. The subjects are about 300 youths each from Japan, the United States, and Germany between the ages of eighteen and twenty-four. Its objective was to clarify the youths' outlook on rules and human relations necessary to carry out daily life. The author was in charge of the survey.

8. Tamotsu Sengoku and Kiichiro Iinaga, *Nihon no Shogakusei* [Japanese primary school children] (Tokyo: NHK Press, 1979), p. 115. The book deals with different ways of scolding that exist in Japan and the United States based on survey findings by the Japan Youth Research Institute in 1979. The subjects were fourth, fifth, and sixth graders, about 200 from each country. Their daily lives and values are examined.

9. The Volvo method is basically intended to give the workers more chances to know the totality of the work process in an automobile plant. See the following book for discussion from the Volvo management perspective: P. G. Gyllenhamer, *People at Work* (Reading, Mass.: Addison-Wesley, 1977).

10. "Consciousness and Character of Top Management," *The Monthly Recruit*, June 1980, p. 35. This is an attitude survey of top management of about seventy corporations in Japan by the survey department of Recruit Center. It elucidates the attitudes of the Japanese managers.

11. This is a kind of *shakun*. Most large Japanese companies have either a *shakun* or *shaze* or both. *Sha* means company. *Kun* means precept. Therefore, *shakun* is a statement of basic precepts of exhortations directed at company employees. *Ze* means what is right or justification. *Shaze* means, then, a statement of corporate principles and ideals and loosely corresponds to the motto of a Western corporation. The original is usually written in brush calligraphy, framed, and hung in the president's office or the board conference room. At some companies, it is customary for the employees to recite in unison the *shakun* or *shaze* every morning before starting work.

12. Shichihei Yamamoto, *Nihon Shihonshugi no Seishin* [The spirit of the Japanese capitalism] (Tokyo: Kobunsha, 1979), p. 24.

13. David C. McClelland, *The Achieving Society* (Princeton: Van Nostrand, 1961).

CHAPTER 7. EGOISTIC SELF-ACTUALIZATION

1. Kunio Odaka, *Shokugyo Shakaigaku* [Occupational sociology] (Tokyo: Iwanami Shoten, 1941). Odaka views occupation from three aspects: income, social responsibility, and self-actualization. Survey on the objective of working is often conducted on these three aspects.

2. Prime Minister's office Youth Bureau, *Occupational Orientation of the Youth—Comparative Study of the Youth between Japan and the U.S.* (Tokyo: Prime Minister's Office Press, 1980), p. 170. The survey was commissioned to

the Japan Youth Research Institute by the Prime Minister's office, Youth Bureau, in March 1980. The subjects were Japanese and American youth, high school students, college students, and working youth (870 Japanese and 537 American). The survey focused on the occupational values of the youths in the two countries.

3. N. C. Morse and R. S. Weiss, "The Function and Meaning of Work and the Job," *American Sociological Review* 20 (April 1955): 192.

4. Ryoichi Iwauchi, *Shokugyoseikatsu no Shakaigaku* [Sociology of occupational life] (Tokyo: Gakubunsha, 1975), pp. 15–16.

5. Original Japanese here is *honne* (true intention) and *tatemae* (attitudinal expression). Japanese mentality has often been called that of ambivalence. Ambivalence is also observed in the Western culture as the idea of diplomatic language shows, which means to help smooth relationships with others. In the case of the Japanese, their ambivalence differs from it because their culture values humbleness. Westerners seem to have ambivalent feelings about it. "That man doesn't disclose his *honne*" is an expression Japanese businessmen use when talking about a rough negotiator on the other side. He may not be obstinate because he wants to be but because, under certain circumstances, he has to emphasize his company's *tatemae*.

When the *tatemae* and the *honne* are the same, there is no problem. But sometimes it happens that they are at variance with each other. The negotiation then becomes an exercise in trying to find a way to satisfy the *honne* without compromising the *tatemae*, at least on the surface.

Excessive adherence to *tatemae*, of course, is often used as a ploy to gain a better bargaining position. The reluctance to reveal the *honne* and to stick ostensibly to *tatemae* also occurs in private social relations, especially when the *honne* is not a very laudable one.

6. Daniel Yankelovich, *The Changing Values on Campus: Political and Personal Attitudes of Today's College Students* (New York: Washington Square Press, 1972).

7. The report of the "First Attitude Survey of the World Youth" by the Prime Minister's office, Youth Bureau, commissioned to the Japan Youth Research Institute. The survey is conducted every five years (1972, 1977, and 1982) with subjects from eleven countries: Brazil, France, India, Japan, Philippines, Sweden, Switzerland, the United Kingdom, the United States, West Germany, and Yugoslavia. The subjects are 2,000 youths from each country, between ages fifteen and twenty-four. It is a survey intended to clarify the attitudes and activities in the areas of school, workplace, home, and life in general.

8. In order to get a job, some college students wear uniforms to job interviews to give an impression that they are serious students. As long hair for male students was regarded as a sign of rebellion, some students cut their hair before appearing for job interviews. There was a marked change in the student attitude after the oil crisis.

Index

Absenteeism, 47, 51; among American workers, 6–7, 10, 11, 13, 14, 15; blue collar vs. white collar, 10; among British workers, 6, 10, 11, 13, 14, 15; causes of, 15; company buses and, 7; among factory workers, 6–7, 10, 11, 13, 14, 15; family life and, 15, 54, 125; firing as deterrent for, 129; at General Motors plant, 71; among Japanese white collar workers, 6, 10; sickness as cause of, 15; wages and, 53; white collar vs. blue collar, 10
Afro-Americans, 37
Alcoholism, 52; among workers, 46, 47
American workers. See Workers, American
American Workers Are As Good, 69
Anxiety, role in motivation to work, 74
Ataka Sangyo, 72
Automobile production, 18–19; American, 37; Japanese vs. American, 21; technology and, 22

Blue collar workers, 6, 27; absenteeism, among, 10; American vs. Japanese, 28
Bonus system, 6, 33–34
Bosses, 12
Breathalyzer, 47
Buses: company, absenteeism and, 7; in Japan, 8; school, 6

Circuits, integrated, 19
Clerical workers, female, 124
College graduates: attitudes toward work, male vs. female, 123; female, reason for working, 123, 134
Computers, as foreman, 44
Crime: in Japan, 73; unemployment and, 72–73; in the United States, 73

Drug addiction, 71, 73

Economic stability, as motivation to work, 5
Education, in Japan, 116, 152
Employment: life-time, 5, 96, 126; part-time, 4
England. See Great Britain
English workers. See Workers, British
European Economic Community, 116

Factory, organization, 20
Family life: absenteeism and, 15, 54, 125; money management in, 97–99; stability of, 110
Female workers, *yaruki* and Japanese, 16
Firing, 41, 50–51; procedures for, 12; threat of, as deterrent for absenteeism, 129; of workers, 58. See also Workers: dismissal of
Foreman: American, 27; change in

About the Author

TAMOTSU SENGOKU, a respected Japanese scholar and writer, is the Managing Director of the Japan Youth Research Institute and a lecturer at Waseda University. He is the author of numerous books and articles on the sociology of youth, employment, schooling, and related subjects.